I0045586

NOT JUST TALENT

THE MILLENNIALS REDEFINING TALENT & HUMAN CAPITAL MANAGEMENT

BY PHILIPE BRUCE

DISCLAIMER

© COPYRIGHT 2016 - ALL RIGHTS RESERVED.

P.O.D.S.
Coaching, LLC

P.O.D.S. Coaching, LLC

PO BOX 24344,

Omaha, NE

68124

ISBN-13: 978-0-9983695-1-8

This document is geared towards providing exact and reliable information in regards to the topic and issue covered.

The information provided herein is stated to be the author's truthful and consistent point of view, in that any liability, in terms of inattention or otherwise, by any usage or abuse of any policies, processes, or directions contained within is the solitary and utter responsibility of the recipient reader. Under no circumstances will any legal responsibility or blame be held against the publisher for any reparation, damages, or monetary loss due to the information herein, either directly or indirectly.

Respective authors own all copyrights not held by the publisher.

The information herein is offered for informational purposes solely, and is universal as so. The presentation of the information is without contract or any type of guarantee assurance.

The trademarks that are used are without any consent, and the publication of the trademark is without permission or backing by the trademark owner. All trademarks and brands within this book are for clarifying purposes only and are the owned by the owners themselves, not affiliated with this document.

To my Parents,

Jacques and Aimée,

who by example taught me the power of faith.

CONTENTS

INTRODUCTION

In the year 2015, the millennials left Generation X behind to become the largest population in the American workforce. By the end of March 2015, the millennial workforce in America stood at a proud 53.5 million strong.[1]

With more and more young people entering the job market, recruiting and effectively utilizing the members of the young Generation Y has become an uphill task for businesses. This has given rise to a problem:

There are millions of job positions that remain vacant while a major chunk of millennials have a hard time building their career.

There are no two opinions on the fact that the millennials are nothing like the generations that preceded them. The general misconception labels them as lazy, non-serious, narcissistic, and of course, job hoppers. With that in mind, most employers tend to overlook the talent and value they bring to the table that could actually prove significant for their business if given a chance.

---

[1] http://www.pewresearch.org/fact-tank/2015/05/11/millennials-surpass-gen-xers-as-the-largest-generation-in-u-s-labor-force/

This book is an attempt to change or at least improve this scenario. Generation Y may be different, but it's not impossible to deal with. The situation only calls for the implementation of effective strategies that allow businesses to capitalize on their Gen Y human capital for collective growth and success of the organization as a whole.

However, before one could begin on that, it is essential to acquire an in-depth knowledge of the situation. This includes understanding the millennials, how they work, what they expect and want from their careers, and the current global scenario of human resource management across organizations.

This book will discuss all of this in detail in addition to providing viable solutions and strategies to employ in order to get the best of the latest addition to the workforce.

The first part of the book will define the issue and actively set a very realistic stage. You will fall right smack into the middle of the harsh social perceptions of the millennials, their reality, and their surroundings. This background is needed to help later on with devising the appropriate solutions.

Let's begin!

SECTION 1: THE MILLENNIALS

Like we said, we aren't getting anywhere without a thorough understanding of the millennial – this section will focus on providing an insight on who they are, what makes them different, and how they fit/gel in the modern corporate world.

WHO ARE THE MILLENNIALS?

Generation Y, Next Generation, or the Millennials are the demographic faction immediately after Generation X. The term millennial is applied to the group of people who attain adulthood around the beginning of the 21st century.

The term first appeared in the book *Generations: The History of America's Future, 1584 to 2069*[2] written by William Straus and Neil Howe back in 1991. According to them the millennial generation includes individuals born between the years 1982 and 2004. However, this delineation varies from source to source.

An article in Time Magazine pegged the millennials between 1980 and 2000.[2] On the contrary, the Newsweek Magazine placed the millennials between 1977 and 1994.[2] Overall, if we round up the earliest and latest birth date propositions for the millennials coming

---

[2] http://www.newsweek.com/now-its-time-generation-next-162866

in from different sources, the millennials belong to the period beginning from 1976 and ending at 2004.

Considering that range, this demographic cohort should be aged between 12 and 40 in the year 2016. The fact that there is immense variation within this generational legion, it is important to observe the Gen Y characteristics in a broader spectrum of environment and that influences their behavior and inclination when it comes to culture, workplace, and technology. We shall be doing just that in the next chapter.

Coming of age in a time of global crises, the millennial generation has been exposed to societal upheaval, perpetual chaos on the global front, and intense economic uncertainty. These circumstances have shaped them to face a myriad of challenges while simultaneously looking for opportunities to capitalize on. They may seem laid back and uninterested, but this generation has had it tough since the beginning. They are aware of the social, economic, religious, and political crises faced by nations on a national and international level – and they are owning it.

According to the US Census Bureau the Millennials are the biggest generation in the U.S. history, with their count reaching a staggering 83.1 million in June 2015.[3] Plagued with problems like lower levels of employment and student loan repayments, these millennials find

[3] http://www.census.gov/newsroom/press-releases/2015/cb15-113.html

themselves burdened with debt and less money to spend than the generations preceding them.

This tech savvy generation may have revolutionized the world of online businesses and retailing; however, when it comes to other luxuries in life – their priorities are more inclined towards bringing social changes and doing what they love. Talking about the greater responsibilities of marriage and family, their attitudes vastly differ from the previous generations mainly because they do not possess the financial means to support any. Some would say that's smart. With the social and economic predicaments prevailing on the global front, thinking of a family when you can't afford a house for yourself would be imprudent unless you live in some parts of Europe. However, looking further into the cause, it's unfair to them that the current Human resource management process in organizations is not adept enough to meet the challenges of hiring millennials as employees.

While we would be discussing that in further chapters, it is important to mention at this stage that the millennials are set to be the most educated generation in the history. With the amount of knowledge and talent they possess, it's a loss on the organization's part to be unable to acclimatize their environments for the millennials –because whether you want it or not, we are moving towards a millennial economy, and their number is only going to rise in the coming years.

They may have been born plugged and wired to the technology, but that's not the only thing that sets the millennials apart from the generations before them. The fact that they are full of contradictions is only a matter of their age. The millennials are different – they have an approach different than their (grand) parents (the baby boomers) for almost everything they do or undertake.

They have trouble accepting norms simply because at the time they are advancing into adulthood, the society itself has undergone a great deal of progression and advancement – and the proliferation of technology is just one of them. As the millennials set themselves to overtake the positions left for them by generations preceding them, they are making the differences between them and their ancestors more prominent.

For a better understanding of the millennials and how they go about things, it is important to understand the contrast that sets them apart from their parent generation.

MILLENNIALS ARE MORE REBELLIOUS

Millennials do not appreciate being confined by rules and guidelines. That obviously doesn't make for a generation of hooligans. Millennials are defying societal norms mainly because they are unable to reason the road mapped out for them by the generations before them. They may be the most educated generation of the century, but how would the society justify the tedious 9 to 5 working hours where they don't end up saving anything because whatever they earn has to be paid off to return their student debt.

MILLENNIALS ARE MORE OPEN-MINDED

Religion, ethnicity, sexual orientation – there are a series of other controversial topics over which the population of the United States divides into conflicting standpoints. Whether it is gay marriage, legalization of marijuana, religious views, or immigration policies, millennials are found to be far more accepting of the diversity than their baby boomer parents. Also a majority of the millennials do not claim affiliation with any religion at all.

MILLENNIALS ARE GOVERNED BY TECHNOLOGY

This may seem repetitive, but without the mention of technology this section would be incomplete. For this generation, nothing happens without technology. They want to promote a cause; they'll do it through Facebook instead of going out on the streets. If they want to meet someone somewhere, they'll simply text the person to show up for a meeting, unlike their parents who would've trusted the other person to be at the decided place on the decided time. Ever wondered why there are so less face-to-face conversations now? It's because these millennials say what they want to on their social profiles, not face to face.

MILLENNIALS ARE MORE OPTIMISTIC

Even with most things not going their way and growing up in a time of political and economic turmoil across the world, a large majority of millennials have 'hope' for a better future. They believe that their economic position would improve in the near future, with more jobs being created and allowing them to pursue their dreams.[4]

MILLENNIALS ARE ALWAYS LOOKING FOR MORE

Unfortunately, millennials have been brought up in a way that they are seldom content with what they have. With everything being provided to them since the day they are born, millennials have developed a habit of always wanting more than what they already have. This is a striking contrast to how the baby boomers were conditioned by their parents. They had to "work hard" to get something they wanted and be thankful for what they had.

MILLENNIALS DON'T SHY AWAY FROM TAKING RISKS

This stems in context with their rebellious nature. Where the baby boomers had career paths defined for them as doctors, engineers, lawyers, accountants, etc. the millennials are not afraid of walking on career paths less taken. They are mostly driven by passion and want jobs in which they feel they can make the most

---

[4] https://www.timeout.com/chicago/things-to-do/what-millennials-are-hopeful-about

difference. They aspire to be professional chefs, artists, curators, and hairstylists; as long as it's something they love doing.

MILLENNIALS PREFER LIVING IN THEIR PARENTS' HOMES

In 2014, the number of youngsters living with their parents reached its highest point since post World War II living arrangements. Almost 32% of youngsters between the age of 18 and 32 (the millennials) chose living with their parents over any other form of living arrangement.[5] This major drift from the ways of their ancestors can be traced back to the lack of finances that have come to define the Generation Y.

MILLENNIALS ARE NOT WELL OFF

With most millennials preferring to stay in the nest, it is no surprise that the percentage of millennial home owners reveal a bleak comparison to the number of baby boomers who owned their own homes by the time they were 30. However, wrapping the issue by labeling the millennials as lazy and unfocused would be unfair. According to a survey, about 64% of the millennials

---

[5] http://www.pewsocialtrends.org/2016/05/24/for-first-time-in-modern-era-living-with-parents-edges-out-other-living-arrangements-for-18-to-34-year-olds/

admitted that owning their own home is *'very important'* to them.[6]

Although, paying off student loans, lack of jobs in the market, their unique work style, and different priorities have made the millennials a less affluent generation. Today's 30-year-olds are far less likely to own homes or cars than their parents at the same age. It cannot be termed a fault entirely on the part of the millennials. The blame has to be shared with the political and economic conditions and the way their baby boomer parents have shaped their lives.

MILLENNIALS ARE PUTTING OFF MARRIAGE AND RESPONSIBILITIES

Most people would consider this yet another way millennials are trying to avoid the reality of life in an attempt to 'have it easy', but what they tend to ignore is the fact that the millennials do not have the resources to support a family. With most of them not having a house of their own, a sustainable job, or the money to support a complete living, it would be foolish for these youngsters to think of marriage and family.

Just like any other generation from the past, the millennials too have their strengths and weaknesses.

[6] http://www.newgeography.com/content/002919-millennials%E2%80%99-home-ownership-dreams-delayed-not-abandoned

This educated, diverse, and liberal group of people holds the potential to bring positive change to the society as a whole. While the baby boomers and the Generation X may not be prepared to absorb the drastic transformation of the society at the hands of the millennials, one cannot ignore the fact that the coming years are going to be all about the millennials only – it's either their way or the highway.

We have already established that the millennials are nothing like the generations before them. They are the change. They are the future. By 2025, Generation Y will constitute around 75% of the workforce across the globe.[7] This generation is set to rule the corporate world in the coming years, much to the discomfort of the *"old boys' club"*.

The millennials play by their own rules. They do not settle for the answers provided to them. These traits make them actual game changers which do not work well for most of the Generation X (current bosses). The general Generation X mindset labels the millennial workforce as stubborn, spoiled, lazy, and entitled – simply because these youngsters reject their way of working.

That does not however mean that the millennials are actually spoiled and lazy. The millennials are free souls. They do not like being confined to something/some place. This is a major reason why this generation rallies against the conventional corporate culture. A 9 to 5 jobs, suits, ties and pencil skirts, and defined work schedules – everything is considered to be a barrier in the way of expressing their creativity and intelligence. Adulthood for this generation is only the beginning of the freedom they are looking for.

---

[7] http://www.cnbc.com/2014/01/22/to-bosses--gen-y-to-dominate-by-2025.html

To understand the millennial workplace philosophy, one needs to closely scrutinize the things that define and drive this generation. These youngsters wear an *'I don't give a #*@%'* attitude and usually do not think twice before quitting their jobs, but that does not make them foolish or any less smart. They may not be ready to accept things the way they come, but they will not even sit around and complain about them – they will go out and change it, or at least try to change it.

That's a troublesome prospect for the corporate members of Generation X. With employees who do not fear the risk of inviting trouble and are out to change the system, most organizations face problems coming to terms with the rapidly changing workplace dynamics.

So what exactly drives them?

Generation Y is big on passion. They are creative and innovative. They are more into things that inspire them or make them happy. Most would prefer a career that pays a little less

– Sometimes not even their bills and debts – as long as it is something they love doing. This is one reason why the millennials are sometimes not interested in the monetary and non- monetary perks offered by companies as a motivational compensation for employees.

But that's not everything that makes this bloc of employees different. Millennials have been found to keep away from office politics – they mind their own business. But if there is a cause they believe in, the same people do not back down from a good fight. They may not be too enthusiastic about workplace ethics, but they do have morals and the thirst to live each day in a fulfilling manner.

In 2014, Deloitte conducted a Millennial Survey that revealed that 56% of the millennial workforce actually ruled out even considering an organization for possible employment based on the organization's values. Also, almost 49% of these millennials said that they refused to undertake a task because they found it to be against their principles.[8]

When they want something – a pay raise or flexible hours – employers can trust them to be direct about it. This generation is educated and apt with technology; it makes them a valuable asset for modern day organizations striving to make their mark amid cut-throat competition. Being street and book smarter than any other generation before them, this generation lives on experiences instead of bank statements. They are not after the positions higher up the ladder; they're more interested in delivering the best of their abilities to the organization they work for while doing something they are passionate about.

Rejecting all the traditional forms of compensations offered to them by companies the millennials have the

[8] http://www2.deloitte.com/global/en/pages/about-deloitte/articles/millennialsurvey.html

modern day organizations in a fix. The question is *"What does the millennial workforce want?"*

CONTINUOUS LEARNING

The millennials are a generation of intellects. During the course of their formal education they are nurtured with learning. Stepping into the corporate world halts the continuous process of learning for most of them. They are not looking for raises in salaries or non- monetary benefits to motivate them for better performance; neither are they interested in climbing the corporate ladder.

What they are looking for is progress and learning – something that saves them from getting stagnant. Most millennials are attracted to organizations that offer regular trainings, certifications, employee development programs to cultivate their workforce; but also let them put their skills to use in the organization.

FLEXIBLE WORK SCHEDULES

The fact that millennials haven't given up on what we term as one of the worst job markets the history has seen is proof that this generation is not lazy. But they are choosy. Most millennials do not wish to work the conventional working hours, they prefer having it their way. They are looking for flexibility – the flexibility to work from home or leniency in the starting and ending time of their work shift.

Millennials believe that the measure of productivity shouldn't be based on the number of hours worked but on the actual quantity and quality of work delivered. They are looking to strike a balance between their work, fun, and passions. They want to make the most of their time on this planet and a little flexibility in the hours doesn't seem like they're asking too much.

GREATER GOOD

The Millennial Survey conducted by Deloitte back in 2014 also revealed that a majority of millennials measured corporate success on the basis of the positive impact on the society brought by the organization – with 63% of them valuing product and service quality higher than other factors.[9]

Millennials have also been charitable and active in supporting local causes across the world. Despite their meager financial positions, these young people have been seen regularly donating and volunteering at different community organizations to bring a positive impact on the surroundings. Hence, when they look for possible employers, the millennials prefer being a part of an organization that supports good causes and works improving the surroundings along with providing quality products and services.

Many members of the Generation X would consider the millennials to be demanding, but if incorporating these little-big changes can change the way organizations do business for the good, then why not? Besides, since the

[9] http://www2.deloitte.com/global/en/pages/about-deloitte/articles/millennialsurvey.html

coming years will see an increase in the number of millennials in the workplace, it is only wise for organizations to mold themselves for what the future holds – and that's exactly what this book is about.

It's better to let these youngsters work from 10 to 10 and reap the benefits of their creativity rather than debating on the 9 to 5 pointlessly and losing out on potential talent – because the millennials are not stopping for anyone. These people don't have much to lose and they will continue with their "YOLO" attitude towards life and keep striving for what's valuable to them.

Now that we've described the millennials and their way of life – both personal and professional, it is time to take a look at the corporate environment these millennials are entering into.

SECTION 2: ORGANIZATIONS AND TALENT MANAGEMENT

The current day job market is widely termed as the worst of its kind throughout the "modern" history. *Why?* There are jobs available, and more keep sprouting up every now and then. However, even with the steady growth in the number of jobs available, the unemployment rates remain stagnant and the (post-recession) compensation levels have dipped down to a historic low *(CNN Money Research Study 2015)*[10].

While the low wage rates are an entirely different subject, it is important to notice that even with the available jobs the job market is unable to bring down the unemployment rates in the country. From October 2015 to July 2016, the United States unemployment rate has seen only a slight decrease of 0.2%.[11] This effectively included 8% of the 18 to 29-year-olds unemployed as of February 2016.[12]

Most economic gurus blame this gap on the ineffective talent management by companies. We're already aware of the fact that employers are reluctant to hire the *'lazy'*,

[10] http://money.cnn.com/2015/01/09/news/economy/wages-raise/

[11] http://www.tradingeconomics.com/united-states/unemployment-rate

[12] https://www.atr.org/millennials-generation-financial-chaos

'non-serious' millennials for permanent positions in their companies. *But are the millennials really at fault?*

Let us first understand the concept of talent management for better understanding of the situation.

WHAT IS TALENT MANAGEMENT?

The term *'talent management'* covers the competency, capability, and authority of an organization's employees. The parameters of this concept stretch beyond hiring the right candidate for the right job at the right time. Talent management further explores the unusual and hidden individuality of a company's employees and ways to nurture these traits for obtaining desired result for the organization.

Using talent management, recruiting the best industry talent is often the top most priority for most organizations. However, retaining that same talent and devising effective strategies to make it transition into the organization's culture happens to be a bigger challenge that companies face while managing talent.

Hence talent management can be summarized as the continuous process of sourcing, recruiting, nurturing, promoting, and retaining talent in the organization while simultaneously meeting organization goals and requirements. For example: Your company wants to acquire the best talent employed at their competitor firms. To accomplish that, they need to offer these people something that they cannot resist – something that persuades them to quit their current job, join your company, and stay there.

If you carefully notice, the example did not mention hiring alone; talent management is a continuous comprehensive process that controls the entry and exit of an employee in addition to getting things done by him for the entire duration of their service.

Often people confuse the talent management function with the human resource management function of the organizations. They may outwardly seem similar, but both these functions have distinct features that set them apart from each other.

So what makes these functions different?

TALENT MANAGEMENT VS HUMAN RESOURCE MANAGEMENT (HRM)

The HR department previously had the centralized charge of hiring, training, and retaining employees. Today, most of these duties have been federated through talent management to the managers who are actually in charge of the said employees. Talent management basically holds the entire organization responsible for these activities.

Human resource management and talent management are like tracking attendance vs. professional development. The HR department observes a more administrative role. It deals with employee benefits, leaves and vacations, complaints, and pay. Talent management on the contrary, is solely focused on improving and promoting organization's best talent.

Lastly, talent management takes a strategic approach in its function. Its strategies and plans are applied throughout the organization and are devised in close coordination with the overall long-term goals of the business. HRM on the other hand, has a tactical approach. It is usually managing employees on a day-to-day basis.

Talent management in an organization can vary in scope and initiatives depending on the size and the priorities of a company. It could just be a simple annual interview of current employees that discusses their strengths and weaknesses and the developmental requirements that can help them improve or it could be a meticulous on-going process that evaluates employees against the long-term initiatives of the company by establishing short term goals that are often reviewed. However, a proper talent management procedure would include the following elements:

RECRUITING THE RIGHT PERSON FOR THE RIGHT JOB

Through talent management organizations are able to properly ascertain the strengths and skills of the employees. Mapping these competencies and skills allows the organization to take into account the inventory of skills currently present within the organization. This is how they are able to take strategic decisions of deploying the right person for the right job and increasing the overall productivity of the employee and the organization as a whole. It also helps create job satisfaction for the employees when their jobs are aligned with their skills and interests.

RETAINING THE COMPANY'S BEST TALENT

An organization is only as capable as the employees it recruits. Therefore, it is crucial for companies to retain good talent within the organization that can help them promote growth and leadership in the market. Companies that do not retain top talent tend to lose out to their competitors. The talent management process includes effective planning and strategies that are designed to develop quality people, acknowledge their performance, and reward them with career growth that makes them stick to the company.

QUALITY HIRING

The quality of a company is directly proportionate to the quality of its workforce. To muster up talent on the top levels of the organization, it is important to hire talent at the bottom levels that can progress their way upwards in the hierarchy. This is a major reason why hiring assessments, training, and talent management programs have become a crucial part of HR processes lately.

UNDERSTANDING THE EMPLOYEES

Under talent management, organizations tend to conduct regular employee assessments that open up gates to deeper insights into the individual career aspirations, developmental needs, likes and dislikes, skills and abilities, and strengths and weaknesses of each employee. Therefore, it gets easier for organizations to harness the individual competencies of each employee for the mutual benefit of the organization and its workforce.

IMPROVING PROFESSIONAL DEVELOPMENT

Talent management helps identify the high potential employees in the organization (Fast Track). This identification allows companies to make better informed investment decisions in the growth, succession, and performance management of their employees and ensuring the optimum utilization of their resources that will eventually bring the desired results if the talent is retained.

It's no secret; for an organization to reach the next level, it needs the people who could take it there. Accomplishing organizational goals that measure success, it is vital for companies to recognize the talent that can actually drive the organization to achieve its set targets.

However, it is important to bear in mind that the skills, qualifications, competencies, and abilities of a person will not bear fruit for the organization if it places the wrong candidate in the wrong position. Talent management would fail if the organization is unable to employ the top industry talent exactly where they should be. Hence, the talent management mechanism of an organization needs to be strong enough to hold the responsibility of building employees' confidence in the organization in addition to ensuring that the organization is equipped with the best to outperform its competitors.

At this point, we feel it is important to introduce the concept of Human Capital Management (HCM) and how together with talent management this discipline of HRM can help companies grow better.

HUMAN CAPITAL MANAGEMENT (HCM) AND TALENT MANAGEMENT

Just like talent management, human capital management revolves around the employees of the company. Each employee in their own capacity is contributing to the combined accomplishment of the company's objectives.

Over the course of their tenure at an organization, employees learn more and gain further experience and exposure that increases their overall productivity and eventually benefits the industry. Employees are often termed as human capital for organizations.

Why?

It's because organizations invest time and money to train and polish employees who in turn, contribute to the overall success of the business.

Human capital management is the management of employees in order to increase their individual productivity and enhance their contribution to the organization they're a part of. The process of human capital management includes effectively acquiring and training employees for increased efficiency.

For most, the concepts of human capital management and talent management may appear to be the same. It's true that both these concepts do overlap at some point, but where HCM deals with the effective management of the employees' skills; talent management is more focused on bringing in, developing, and retaining talented individuals in the organization while making sure their talent is put to the right use.

THE EVOLUTION OF HUMAN RESOURCE MANAGEMENT

Over the last fifty years, the Human Resource philosophy and role in organizations has undergone a complete transformation. What originally started as the 'International Labor Relations' was later changes to *'Personnel'* only to be called the *"Human Resources"* like we know it today.

During the entire time, it wasn't just the name that changed. In fact, the human resource function went from being a support function for an organization to an actual strategic function as the role of this particular department evolved.

Where in the past the HR department was famous for being the gatekeeper and policy enforcer for the organization, it has now assumed the role of being the employee and management facilitator and a consultant on devising policy strategies. Human resource departments overall have become proactive forums focused on the betterment of the organizational culture and the success of its mission.

For the longest of times, the concept of talent management did not exist. Everything related to the employees was dealt by the Human Resource department of the organization. Back then, even with the changing times and markets the competition was stringent but sustainable. Hence, there was no need for the appropriate management of talent within a company.

It was during the economic downfall and instability in the 1990s *(continuing to the early 2000s)* that set the dominoes crashing across the world that businesses found themselves in a race against time for survival. With the money not coming in, the redundancy rates going up, and cut-throat competition for survival businesses had to look for in-house solutions to keep going.

Out came the concept of talent management, whereby businesses started mapping the talents of their existing employees while simultaneously attracting the cream employees from the competitors in an attempt to outperform the latter. But acquiring talent alone wasn't going to work – so businesses had to make sure the talent they had and the limited new talent they could acquire was put to the right use.

It's been more than two decades that the term *'talent management'* was first used as a function of human resource management. It has now developed into a knowledge-based, highly consultative function of effective human resource management in organizations. The principle has been simple since its inception: enabling organizations to focus on drawing the top talented people and retaining them.

It basically provides a company with the ability to have the best workforce on board to meet the needs of its business. However, there are two fundamental parameters always fluctuating that require subsequent re-evaluation of the whole idea of talent management on a regular basis:

- **Technology:** With the proliferation of technology, the collective capabilities of the

  businesses and its employees have radically expanded over the years and will continue so in the coming years.

- **Business circumstances:** The business dynamics and trends keep changing all the time and demand upgrades in the roles of talent and business managers for improved coherence with the modern business world.

Today, the talent management premise is an embodiment of administrative solutions that are having a positive impact on all-round aspects of the organization's operations. Companies that have made the paradigm shift of separating talent management from the human resource function are now more capable of gathering an effective workforce that is up to meet the challenges of the modern business world.

From an insignificant function to one of the most critical HR activities, talent management has undergone drastic changes over time. With the concept evolving for the better every day, it is important to analyze the latest trends that govern the talent management function in modern organizations.

THERE'S A WAR OUT THERE - THE WAR OF TALENTS

The biggest challenge HR management across the globe faces is discovering and retaining the top talent in their respective organizations. There is no divergence on part of the HR survey consultancies when they say that organizations across the world face a deficiency of talented employees and retaining the ones they have is often more difficult than it seems. Also, there have been research, which reveal that effective and efficient management of talent within an organization improves the overall productivity of the company. [13] Thus, companies out there all strive to attract and retain the cream talent of the industry – often residing to policies that potential talents find hard to resists. *It's all about the policies!*

BALANCING TALENT AND TECHNOLOGY

Organizations that have been quick to adapt technology in their human capital management programs have been

---

[13] http://www.sci-int.com/pdf/202512997537-637-642-Aiza-TM%20&%20OE-Sci%20Int-GP-Final.pdf

found to be far more apt in promoting and polishing the talent they acquire and/or employ. An increasing amount of organizations are now developing online portals to provide employees with a convenient platform to manage their careers and have easier access to the assorted schemes and benefits provided by the organization. These portals are also helping organizations gain a better understanding of their employees, their needs, aims, and aspirations.

INTERNAL TALENT AND THE SKILL POOLS

Sometimes, organizations hire people who possess the skills, abilities, and requirements of the vacant post in the organization. Having that talent pass through their talent management process, organizations invest in the development and learning of these employees; and simultaneously provide them with progressive career goals and increased opportunities for job satisfaction. This is how they make sure that the talent they hire and put money on stays with them for a longer time.

However, there is an additional function organizations undertake with respect to the talent they employ. Hiring talented people creates a pool of skills and abilities within the organization, and at times certain skills and abilities are better suited for a post different than the one they're employed for. Modern day talent management identifies what skills within the skills inventory of the organization would be fit for which internal succession. This helps companies empower their employees and resultantly themselves too.

THE GLOBAL POPULATION CRISES

Statistics show that the world is rapidly moving towards a demographic catastrophe [14]. Currently the world population is either young or over 60. A 2015 world demographic publication by the US revealed that over-60 is the fastest aging population group across the world since the year 2000.

Increase in world population relative to 2000, by broad age group, 2000-2050

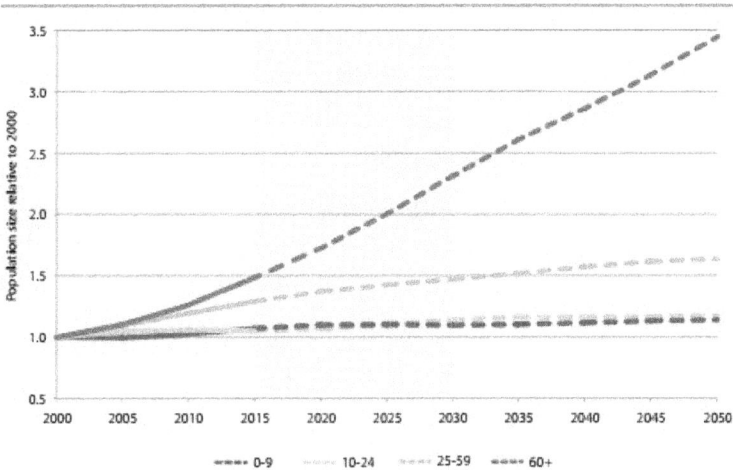

FIGURE 1

By the year 2030, the same population faction is expected to grow by another 56%. This demographic

14

http://www.un.org/en/development/desa/population/publications/pdf/ageing/WPA2015_Highlights.pdf

situation is an alarming factor for human capital managers. With a significant dearth of workers expected in the near future, human capital managers need to be on their toes to employ strategies and policies that help them maximize their talent retention and development.

IMPROVING THE HRM FUNCTION

With its unique dynamics, talent management is helping organizations capitalize on the talent available to them in addition to improving the overall human resource management function. Modern day HRM is required to center its attention more on the qualitative aspects of the organization rather than the quantitative aspects related to the employees. Talent management has taken over the quantitative facet of employee management. They are maintaining scorecards, conducting surveys, and undertaking every possible activity to nurture perpetual growth of the organization's employees.

AN OPPORTUNITY TO BECOME THE EMPLOYER OF CHOICE

Proper talent management is helping companies attract the right employees. The concept has become an important contributor to the perceived value of an organization as an employer. Talent management promotes the company's brand value for potential and current employees. Candidates look for growth and development opportunities in the organizations they wish to join. Hence, the better a company's talent management, the more talent it'll attract. It works more or less like a competitive advantage over competitors in the war of talent.

ARE ORGANIZATIONS MANAGING TALENT RIGHT?

We have established the concept of talent management and how it helps organizations improve themselves on the road to accomplishing their long term growth. In an ideal situation, organizations with effective talent management programs should be able to make head way with their productivity and talent retention. However unfortunately, this is not how it is in the real world.

Organizations face a myriad of factors that influence the effectiveness of their talent management programs. It may be weak policies, market conditions, improper implementations, or other impediments that hinder the talent management process for organizations.

Here's a look at what might go wrong for talent management in organizations:

THE HUMAN FACTOR

Research conducted by McKinsey in 2006 revealed that the most common obstacle in effective talent management is the 'human'.[17] It was found that it is the people who fail to execute people management as they should. Most organizations that lack proper talent management either have the top management passing the buck to the line managers for acting irresponsibly when it comes to human capital management or the executive putting the blame of misalignment of talent management and business strategies on the top management.

What companies like these forget is the fact that talent management is not a function limited to a particular department or class of employees in the organization. It is a perpetual process that requires strategic input and priority from every single person in the organization. Of course the policy makers may be the driving force behind its overall effectiveness, but if the line managers don't implement it right or the employees don't take the desired interest in it – the organization is back to square one on this.

THE WORK ENVIRONMENT

Today, the work environment in organizations across the globe is multigenerational. The baby boomers are nearing their retirement, the Generation X is taking up the leadership posts, and Generation Y is entering the market in hopes of making sound thriving careers.

Most companies in this situation find themselves at the crossroads between devising talent management strategies that helps them retain mid-career talent of the Generation X *(as they are departing from organizations where they don't see growth because of the delayed retirements of the generation before them)* and attract the young lot of Generation Y *(who are talented and by far the most educated generation)* to work for them. With the Generation X and the millennials being completely different from each other, there is often a gap in the talent management policies that hamper their effectiveness.

Currently, for organizations Generation X is the breed of employees that they have invested in over time to develop them for leadership succession. Talent management strategies for them will obviously be different from the ones needed to attract and retain the millennials to the organization. Millennials do not follow the norms. A strategy that may work to effectively manage talent for Generation X may fall flat when implemented on Generation Y.

Often organizations fail to strike a balance between the two extremes. This leads to ineffective talent management and the exodus of valuable employees from the organization. Instead of proving fruitful for the business, talent management processes as such become a waste of time, money, and talent for the company.

COMMUNICATION AND EMPLOYEE RELATIONS

Like we mentioned earlier, the process of talent management requires commitment from both ends. The management and the employees both need to be actively involved in the process to guarantee results. To be able to work together properly, it is important that there is adequate communication and a healthy work relationship between both parties. However, it is important for the management to take the first few steps towards creating an environment where the devised strategy for talent management can actually thrive.

Talent management is all about growing as an organization by promoting the best talents. However, if the management of a company is not committed to the cause, even the most talented employees would face a difficult time getting along and/or taking them seriously. This is where communication comes into play.

Communication helps establish better work relation between managers and employees. So whether it's a new recruit or an existing employee who possesses an extraordinary flair for a job different than the one he's currently working on – the corresponding managers should be able to communicate to them exactly what the organization expects from them and the goals they should be working for.

It is also important for the management to be aware of the personal goals and career aspirations of individual employees, only then they can be able to design talent management strategies that are mutually beneficial for both – the employee and the organization.

Most organizations that do not take effective communication between management and employees seriously often see their talent management programs going down the drain. It is important to mention at this point that talent management program for one company may not necessarily work the same way for the other. This process is highly susceptible to industrial norms, market conditions, and organization dynamics, and hence is different for every organization.

Talent management programs are highly susceptible to problems arising from a multitude of reasons. These problems often lead to increase in company expenditure and a subsequent decrease in its revenues. Truth is there will rarely be an organization that does not face problems in the successful planning and execution of their talent management program; but that does not mean they give up on it.

Regardless of the reasons operating behind the malfunction of a well-planned talent management strategy, it is important for organizations to constantly evaluate and re-evaluate their strategy and progress. Simple questions like the one listed below can help you assess the effectiveness of your talent management program.

- What are the most prominent talent-related risks threatening the achievement of organizational goals?

- Is everyone on the same page for the priorities that need to be focused on in order to bridge the skills gap that may arise in the future?

- What measures of progress do we have against the reduction of these risks?

The answers to these questions wouldn't always be in favor of the organization as a whole. This is where the management needs to step in and ensure the smooth functioning of talent management process. An effective talent management system would always avoid the following issues:

UNNECESSARY TURNOVER

After the global economic recession in 2008, organizations saw a sluggish trend in the Baby Boomer retirements. This in turn has led to the high potential Generation X talents in their mid-careers moving towards an exodus from their current organizations. With opportunities for career growth and promotions blocked, they usually don't see a point to staying in the same place. Besides, the ongoing job-hopping of the millennials is yet another concern.

A successful strategy would be one devised to nurture both these brands of talent and make them stay with the organization by creating ample opportunities for them to progress.

INSUFFICIENT EMPLOYEE GROWTH

When an organization invests in the development and grooming of their employees, it has a two-fold impact. One, the company gets to prepare the next breed of leaders that would take over the leadership reigns from the ones before them. Two, it creates a sense of self-actualization, accomplishment, and progress in their employees. If this spending on employees is not generating any of the aforementioned impacts, the organization is not doing the talent management process right.

Inadequate employee development creates a rift between the management and the employees which is compelling enough for even the most loyal employees to look for a switch in jobs or careers.

INAPPROPRIATE PERFORMANCE MANAGEMENT

The whole point of managing talents is to reap the benefits of the best performance of talented employees. Unfortunately, most organizations do not pay attention to managing the performance of their employees.

An extremely important aspect of talent management is to make sure the employees are aware of their responsibilities and are held accountable for it. Unless they're held accountable for it, even the best employees will not think twice of the financial repercussions of poor performance on their part.

Like we said, there needs to be adequate communication of what is expected from them and how they're expected to deliver it.

LACK OF LEADERSHIP SUCCESSION

A good talent management system would be focused on creating leaders for the future. With the Baby Boomers impending retirement, the organizations that haven't invested in preparing the next generation to assume the role of future leaders of the organization have undeniably failed at implementing an effective talent management process.

Without experienced leadership talent available to the organizations, there are slim chances for it to survive the brutal talent war happening right now in the job markets. If anything, talent management programs should be adequately designed to promote the best talent into leadership positions as the organization progresses towards the accomplishment of its goals.

LOSING OUT ON VITAL KNOWLEDGE

Industries like healthcare, energy, aerospace, and others have knowledge intensive backgrounds. These industries employ highly specialized individuals who individually hold troves of complex knowledge. They have years of experience that have pooled into their skills, abilities, and knowledge. When these employees leave, they drain the organization off their expertise and invaluable knowledge.

Hence, a talent management system needs to be able to identify these key employees and the capabilities they add to the organization on an individual basis. These employees need to be adequately managed and retained to maintain the performance of the organization as a whole.

For the talent management program to be successful, it is crucial that its strategy is perfectly aligned with the overall business strategy of the organization. While talent management is a concept widely applicable to all classes of employees, it is the millennials that have the managements of different organizations in a fix about proper human capital management.

The millennials are educated, talented, skilled, and passionate; but at the same time they are rebellious, capricious, and free-spirited. Their unpredictability and defiance makes it difficult to draft an effective strategy to attract and retain them within the same organization.

It may be difficult, but it's not impossible. Over the course of the rest of this book, one can acquire the necessary knowledge required to retain and adequately nourish the millennial talent within the organization.

SECTION 3: THE MILLENNIALS AND HUMAN RESOURCE MANAGEMENT IN ORGANIZATIONS

Talent management combines the concepts of employee engagement and employee retention into a comprehensive process that is not new to anyone anymore. We just discussed the issues organizations face during their talent management processes and the possible course to a proper system for managing talent. However, when it comes to managing the millennials most organizations are clueless.

One can't entirely blame the organizations for lacking the directives and strategies for effectively utilizing this rich source of talents, but with the millennials rapidly becoming the most dominant group of the workforce, it would be rather foolish of the organizations to ignore the impact of not having clearer human capital management strategies to make their organizations gain a competitive edge over others in employing and retaining the best industry talents.

It is evident from everything previously discussed in this book that the millennials do not fit anything conventional. They hate being dictated to and would rather do what they feel like instead of taking orders from someone. So ideally, the policies and strategies that worked wonders for human capital management of baby boomers and the Generation X tend to fall flat for the millennials.

Millennials are the change and they **demand** change at the workplace too. Gone are the days when employees used to mold themselves to fit into the culture of their organization. For the millennials it's the other way round. They'd rather have the entire organizational culture undergo complete transformation than conforming to the norms.

So, if the organization isn't changing according to their work style, they'll simply quit and hunt for an employer that is more 'suited' to them. This goes against the basic principle of employee retention that forms an integral part of effective talent management.

Fortunately, an increasing number of organizations realize the importance of shifting gears to accommodate the capricious work style of the millennials – YES! The millennials are already changing the work environments.

ARE THE MILLENNIALS CHANGING THE WORKPLACE?

There are a number of drastic changes that are helping different organizations adapt better to the millennials. The three most prominent ones are discussed below:

THE TRANSPARENCY

Millennials do not have the habit of settling for anything less than what they want. Millennials are strong advocates of transparency when it comes to official communication. A transparent management for them is one that promotes effective two-way communication between employees and themselves.

Contrary to the concept of organizational hierarchy, transparency encourages managers to focus on introducing comprehensible communication practices and increased managerial availability. Even if it were not for the millennials, the valuable policy is worth implementing for optimizing the work processes and promoting better flow of information.

Take it this way: *Would you rather have your employee walk into your office and inform you about a significant blunder they just made or would you prefer discovering it during an exit interview?*

Transparency allows managers a greater insight into the mind and working style of their employees. It helps both the managers and the employees understand each other better – *we think that's extremely important for a healthy work environment.*

THE SOCIALIZING

Millennials have grown up in the age of technological proliferation and being connected through technology is an indomitable part of their existence. Yes! Social media is part of socializing. Statistics show that there are 56% millennials who turn down job offers from companies that ban the use of social media at the workplace.[15] *Can you imagine the talent companies can deprive themselves off by imposing a ban on social media at work?*

Times are changing and to be able to survive amidst cutthroat competition, organizations need to bend this rule and ensure mobile compatibility in their systems and their cultures and introduce multichannel communications through social media to attract and retain millennial talent. If you ask us, there isn't much companies can do about this stipulation, because by the year 2025, 3 out of every 4 employees would be millennials![16]

THE PERSONAL DEVELOPMENT

Did you know that millennials on an average stay with an organization for not more than 2 years as opposed to the Generation X average of 5 years?

The fact that millennials are difficult to retain is already well established in the job market and organizations are looking for viable solutions to increase this time span to a little longer than 2 years, let's say somewhere between 3 to 4 years at least. For that purpose, it is important to realize what exactly the millennials are after – they don't work for monetary perks or non-monetary benefits.

---

[15] Infographic: 27 Statistics About Millennials in the Workplace

[16] Refer footnote 18

They work for LEARNING!

Millennials are looking for organizations that provide overt opportunities for personal development. When they switch jobs, they usually opt for positions that give them the chance to explore their careers in depth. It is more a matter of self-actualization than moods. Organizations with proper talent management systems, informal and formal learning initiatives, and growth opportunities tend to attract more millennial workforce than ones sticking to the traditional norms of running the business.

Whatever change an organization wishes to make would be futile without the management on board and willing to adapt the new norms and policies. We're talking about a cultural shift in organizational paradigms and it can move in just one direction – top to bottom. So unless the management implements and practices the change themselves, one can't expect the employees to transition.

There are certain things that the management needs to adopt in order to trigger the change that can help attract and retain the millennials in the organization:

REVIEWING DECISIONS

Managers need to be mindful of the level of employees working under their command. These employees can be both Generation X'ers and the millennials. Hence every decision taken should be contextualized for relevance to both these brands of employees. Also, managers need to take steps to invite employee input on managerial matters that can improve the decision-making process and develop a sense of belonging in the employees.

Being granted the ability to contribute to the company-driving decisions and projects with their suggestions will make the employees feel valued and help them at the bigger picture of the organization's goals. *The millennials WANT this!*

EMPOWERING EMPLOYEES

Managers should be prepared to delegate a certain level of autonomy to the employees. They need to trust their instinct and the talents they are managing. Traditionally, most managers wouldn't want to hand over a project to a new recruit, but *what if that new recruit is better at handling and executing this project than anyone else on the team?* One can never know unless you grant them the opportunity to own a project, work on it, and deliver the best of what they've got.

Some may think that empowering employees may undermine the authority of the managers, but this is where the actual change occurs. For real, measurable differences in overall productivity, managers need to take a step back to allow employees do what they are best at. The managers don't *"step down"*, they only assume a position to helps them keep an eye on the overall progress of the work, evaluate the effectiveness of their decisions, make changes where necessary, and focus on the greater impact of their decisions of their decisions on the organization.

STRIKING A BALANCE

It is very important for managers to learn to balance a collaborative agent and granting autonomy. Millennials in the workforce are not looking for the typical **"bosses"**. They do not want someone who would tell them what to do and how to do it. Hence, it is the managers who adopt a coach-like persona that have proven better bosses for the millennials.

When you grant autonomy to your employees, your job does not end. Your employee may require guidance, advanced expertise, and feedback to develop a final product that is exactly what it should be. Managers need to adopt an 'open-door' policy that allows the employees to walk up to them and discuss their issues, brainstorm for solutions, and obtain your feedback.

For traditional managers, these changes may be a bit too much too soon, but the corporate world is fast evolving, and organizations that successfully adapt to this change are the ones winning the talent war over their competitors.

Change being the only constant is an inevitable aspect of our lives. Everything around us is changing all the time and although it seems perfectly natural, making and accepting change often comes as a challenge for most. In order to efficiently utilize the millennial talent, organizations need to change both their managerial practices and their systems.

It is impractical to expect an overnight change, because unlike adopting latest technologies changing management styles and leadership perspectives may cause delays. Making the change is one side of the coin, adapting to that change is a completely different thing. With organizations having multigenerational workforces, acclimatizing to a work environment that is more transparent and more social can prove to be a substantial change for most employee levels.

However, it's a change worth striving for and it's not just about the millennials. Yes, the millennials may have inspired the cultural change, but once it's done organizations can reap the benefits of increased agility, better information mobility, and a reduction in staff-turnover. Organizations shouldn't look at this change as one made for accommodating the new generation of employees. It should be viewed as optimizing the organizational culture and system for the 21st century.

We have been repeating this over and again that the millennials are here to stay – whether you like it or not. There is colossal millennial talent out there in the market waiting to be tapped. Successfully acquiring this talent can gain some serious competitive edge for your organization. Millennials as employees have the skill and knowledge to achieve great milestones for the organization.

The only thing required here is a flexible and supportive management that helps them spread their wings and fly. Also, there have been numerous human capital management tools sprouting up in an attempt to manage this latest breed of employees better. We shall be discussing these tools and techniques in detail over the course of this section.

THE CONCEPT OF ACTIVE PEOPLE ENGAGEMENT (APE)

When it comes to assessing the productivity and overall performance of an organization, the biggest factor undermining it is *wastage* – the waste of resources, efforts, and time. This wastage is common in organizations where the employees are not actively and effectively engaged.

Do you think an organization like that can actually improve its performance when striving to achieve its business objectives?

The answer to that is obviously *'NO'*. Improper management of the workforce leads to underutilization of their talents and consequent losses in terms of time and overheads. Experts have time and again argued that keeping the workforce engaged can win potent competitive advantage for organizations. They remain of the view that companies need to regularly evaluate the level of their people engagement and consequently design behavioral strategies that can optimize this level of engagement.

At this point, one may want to ask:

- *What is meant by active employee management?*

- *What does the inefficient engagement of employees cost the organization?*

- *What can organizations do about it?*

Each of these questions will be dealt with in detail as we proceed with the book.

Active People/Employee Engagement (APE) is the name given to the process whereby companies can ensure that each of their employees is completely involved in and passionate about their work. Tim Rutledge, in his book *Getting Engaged: The New Workplace Loyalty*, defines an engaged employee as

> *"An employee who is committed to, fascinated by, and attracted to the work"*

In short, engaged employees are ones that are cognitively attentive and connected to the organization they work for. Active people management is all about creating employees that place the future of the organization on their priority lists and are keen on putting in the time, talent, and effort required to make the organization successful. Back in 1998, a study named The War for Talent conducted by McKinsey & Co. predicted a deficit of skilled employees in the future – that future is now.[17] The study only went on to prove Rutledge's emphasis on the implementation of adequate retention plans to optimally manage the talent available within the organization.

17

http://www.executivesondemand.net/managementsourcing/images/stories/artigos_pdf/gestao/The_war_for_talent.pdf

It wouldn't be wrong to say that active people engagement is one of the prime concerns for managements across the globe. According to the Employment Engagement Index posted semi-annually by the Gallup Management Journal:

- About 70% of the total workforce in America alone is not actively engaged at work.[18]

- Around 71% of the millennials workforce is actively disengaged at work.[19]

These statistics are alarming and giving the condition of the job markets, it is becoming increasingly imperative for organizations to take immediate measures to train, develop, and retain talent within the organization. That is only possible when their employees are inspired by, dedicated to, and interested in the job they are doing.

During the various surveys conducted across the globe, it was revealed that the engagement levels of employees belonging to the same age-group varied considerably from one country to another. Another important insight into the matter was that the employee engagement levels were not really influenced by the prevailing macro-economic conditions in the country;

---

[18] http://www.gallup.com/services/178514/state-american-workplace.aspx?g_source=EMPLOYEE_ENGAGEMENT&g_medium=topic&g_campaign=tiles

[19] http://www.gallup.com/businessjournal/194204/millennials-job-hoppers-not.aspx?g_source=EMPLOYEE_ENGAGEMENT&g_medium=topic&g_campaign=tiles

rather it was the work culture and experience that greatly impacted the phenomenon.

THE LEVELS OF PEOPLE ENGAGEMENT IN ORGANIZATIONS

When it comes to the millennials, active people engagement has become more of an epidemic for modern organizations. There could be a number of factors influencing the general lack of engagement among employees. It could be attributed to poor management or the misaligned purposes and objectives of the organization.

The engagement level of employees within an organization can be categorized into three different groups:

THE ACTIVELY ENGAGED

Employees that are actively engaged invest their minds and hearts into their work. They strive to achieve the objectives assigned to them for fulfilling the greater purpose of the organization. These employees are definitely an asset for the organization, bringing their A-game in everything they do. It is the active engagement of employees that organizations should aim to achieve.

THE DISENGAGED

For the disengaged employees, work is only a routine. They are not concerned about what collective goals their company wishes to accomplish or the ways in which they as individuals can contribute to the company's objectives. They will only do the work that is assigned to them with the least amount of interest and/or anticipation of better outputs. For the disengaged employees, companies need to take steps to instill engagement into their work styles.

THE ACTIVELY DISENGAGED

By far the worst kinds of employees a company can have are the ones actively disengaged. These employees are far more dangerous than the uninvolved and unproductive breed of disengaged employees. In addition to not caring about the company's progress, these employees direct their efforts into bringing the organization down.

How to identify these employees?

You can find these employees most active in spreading rumors. They like to complain and have a good time poisoning the minds of other engaged employees. This creates an adverse impact on the motivation and performance of other employees in the organization. Now relate all this to the Gallup statistics provided under *The Active People Engagement Crises* and assess the havoc 71% of actively disengaged millennial workforce can wreak on the economy!

Many companies lack the basic concept of employee engagement and the relevant policies that need to be implemented in order to boost the involvement and commitment of their employees. This is a major reason why, these organizations are unable to appropriately deal with and manage the millennials and their talent.

DOES EMPLOYEE ENGAGEMENT REALLY HELP MAKE A DIFFERENCE?

Back in 2013, Gallup conducted a study[20] that revealed that nine different performance outcomes were connected to the level of employee engagement in an organization. These included:

- Productivity

- Profitability

- Turnover

- Product/service quality

- Customer ratings

- Theft (shrinkage)

- Safety incidents

- Absenteeism

- Customer ratings

The study also established employee engagement as a key component of the companies' performances even in times as bad as the economic recessions. However, a

[20] http://www.gallup.com/businessjournal/163130/employee-engagement-drives-growth.aspx

recent Harvard Business Review article[21] introduced an interesting twist to the phenomenon of high engagement levels of employees.

The article does agree that good scores for employee engagement can have a positive impact on the performance, retention, and well-being of the employees and the overall organization; but there's a down side to it. High levels of employee engagement come with a price.

Let's take a look what could possibly be the "bad" part:

According to the article, engaged employees are satisfied with their jobs and like working in their current capacity. They may come up with a number of innovative ideas, but not many of them would take the initiative to challenge the existing parameters in the organizations. The resulting complacence is something that can hinder the company's progress in the long-run.

In an attempt to collect an engaged workforce, organizations may be biased in their hiring processes. Engagement is something that can be both, instilled into an individual or already present in them as a personality trait. It is something more common in extroverts and this

---

[21] https://hbr.org/2016/08/the-dark-side-of-high-employee-engagement?utm_content=socialchampVy7zdzV3Kb&utm_medium=social&utm_source=twitter.com&utm_campaign=socialchamp.io

70

just might compel organizations to give preference to extroverts over the introverts to improve their overall engagement scores. *But what if the introvert that was just passed on was someone more talented and valuable to the organization than the person they hired?*

Also, the process of active people engagement is to train everyone to keep a positive outlook on things in an organization. However, a little amount of negative thinking is necessary to keep things on track, identify loopholes and possible downsides to the way things are. Moderate amounts of work stress can prove beneficial for employee productivity and someone with a pessimistic approach to things may be able to provide a   new vantage point for the organization to look at the challenges it faces.

Lastly, employees that remain highly engaged throughout their workday may experience frequent burnouts. Being highly passionate and enthusiastic about their work, these employees tend to overlook other crucial aspects of their lives – proper rest, health, and   more. Organizations should be able to look at the long-term impacts of their policies.

Short term profits may present an attractive prospect, but for sustainable growth organizations need to look at the combined impact of the policies they adopt. Employee engagement influences the mindsets of employees. They are driven to make a difference, they are confident about their abilities, skills, and knowledge and how they can implement those to create the desired impact. However, when the same employees are pushed too much towards active engagement, things take a downturn in the long run.

To boost engagement scores that bring favorable results companies need to strike a balance between the impacts of positivity and moderate negativity. There are a number of initiatives organizations can employ to boost engagement and productivity in the right manner. These initiatives will be discussed later in the book in complete detail.

They say it's easier said than done – *we agree!* Talking about implementing a balanced active people engagement policy in the organization is far simpler than actually making it happen. Managers have it tough. The process just doesn't begin with gathering the employees in the conference room and lecturing them on the basics of the concept. The phenomenon is far deeper embedded and has to be channeled into the process to help the employees ease into it.

How do managers accomplish that?

Ralph Stayer, the CEO of Johnsonville Sausage led the turnaround in his organization and he has described the entire situation in his book *Flight of the Buffalo: Soaring to Excellence, Learning to Let Employees Lead.*

The book describes that Ralph Stayer noticed that the employees at Johnsonville Sausage were apathetic towards their work. He describes them as 'careless'. These employees were regularly wasting resources, dropping equipment, and defiant in accepting any responsibility for the work they delivered. They worked a monotonous routine – came to work, did the work they were assigned, completed their shift, and left. But this wasn't going anywhere for Johnsonville and Ralph Stayer being the enthusiastic person he was – this proved to be an alarming situation.

Ralph Stayer felt stuck in the role of a babysitter who simply looks over the employees completing their tasks without an ounce of commitment or motivation to do it better. This was the time, Ralph Stayer thought it was impossible to inspire these employees to improve their performance and productivity and the susceptibility of the business' downfall was just too high.

It was in a meeting with communications professor Lee Thayer *(The University of Amsterdam, Harvard Graduate School of Business, Universidad Complutense in Mexico, Queensland University of Technology in Australia, etc.)* that Stayer finally found the solution he was looking for. Thayer made Ralph Stayer realize that one on most prominent tasks of a leader is to be able to create a work environment that allows employees to explore and employ their complete potential. As opposed to the general view, the role of the CEO is not to make their employees listen to what the CEO has to say; rather, it is to set up a proper system that makes these individuals want to listen.

According to Thayer, the combined impact of the right work culture and environment gives rise to wants rather than requirements. This lifts the unnecessary limitations placed over the extent of achievement employees can aim for. Realizing this was his actual calling, Stayer set out to change the way things were in Johnsonville Sausage.

In the book he wrote:

"I learned what I had to do in order to succeed, but I never thought that learning was all that important. My willingness to do whatever it takes to succeed is what fueled Johnsonville's growth. In 1980 I hit the wall. I realized that if I kept doing what I had always done, I was going to keep getting what I was getting. And I didn't like what I was getting. I would never achieve my dream. I could see the rest of my business life being a never-ending stream of crises, problems, and dropped balls. We could keep growing and have decent profits, but it wasn't the success I was looking for."[22]

The first thing Ralph Stayer did was to identify and acknowledge the difference between commitment and compliance. He realized that he needed an engaged workforce in order to achieve the improvement in organizational performance that he was aiming for. Ralph Stayer also realized that if he wanted to bring the change, he had to start with himself. Hence, the CEO of Johnsonville Sausage set to change his leadership style before moving on to the workforce.

Ralph Stayer wanted an engaged workforce – one that delivered stellar performance as and when required from them. But he realized he couldn't achieve that unless he let go the habit of "demanding" it from the

[22] https://www.sumhr.com/employee-retention/

employees or staying on the sidelines when the ship hits the rocks.

Just like Ralph Stayer, organizations' heads and/or management are under constant pressure to improve the overall performance and productivity of the company. This feat cannot be completed without the commitment and cooperation of the workforce. Hence, as important as it is to motivate and inspire the employees, managers shouldn't neglect the fact that they too need to change themselves to trigger the overall turnaround they desire.

Like we mentioned before, modern day managers need to quit their dictatorial stance and take on a more leader-like approach to be able to extract the best out of their employees. This is especially important in the case of organizations that have a majority of their workforce based on the millennials. This generation does not wait around or take orders from anyone. They don't get what they want – they simply leave.

But that doesn't work in the best interests of the organization now, does it?

THE CONCEPT OF ENCOURAGED INTRAPRENEURSHIP

Another important phenomenon for efficient management of human capital is the concept of Intrapreneurship. In simple terms, intrapreneurship occurs when employees within an organization adopt an entrepreneurial way of thinking when performing their assigned roles in the company. This brings us to the next important question:

What is the entrepreneurial way of thinking?

The answer to that can be obtained with a deeper understanding of 'Entrepreneurship'.

The book *Entrepreneurship: Critical Perspectives on Business and Management by Norris F. Krueger* defines entrepreneurship as:

"Entrepreneurship is the process of creating value by bringing together a unique package of resources to exploit an opportunity."[23]

The book *Global Perspectives on Achieving Success in High and Low Cost Operating Environments by Göran Roos* defined entrepreneurship using the definition put together by *Professor Howard Stevenson of the Harvard Business School* as:

"Entrepreneurship is the pursuit of opportunity without regard to resources currently controlled[24] If we closely observe the definitions mentioned above, one thing comes out clear – entrepreneurs are driven by opportunity. These opportunities arise as a result of changing environments and entrepreneurs have the ability to track and observe the patterns of the changing environment.

Unlike managers, entrepreneurs do not plan their endeavors around the availability of resources. Where a manager would ask, *"What can I possibly achieve with the resources available under my control?"* an

---

[23] Entrepreneurship: Critical Perspectives on Business and Management (Page 49)
[24] Global Perspectives on Achieving Success in High and Low Cost Operating Environments (Page 353)

entrepreneur would focus on, *"What resources should I acquire to achieve what I want?"*

So what is the difference between entrepreneurship and intrapreneurship? Let's find out.

HOW IS INTRAPRENEURSHIP DIFFERENT FROM ENTREPRENEURSHIP?

Intrapreneurs are visionary employees who think like entrepreneurs. Within the environmental constraints of the organization they work for. These employees use their creativity and innovation to transform ideas and dreams into measurable gains for the organization and themselves.

Since these employees are driven by opportunities, it is extremely important for organizations to identify them and create a supportive environment that promotes their endeavors. Intrapreneurship fails when intrapreneurs don't find their organizational environment supportive. This usually pushes them to leave the organization and start their own entrepreneurial ventures – *that right there, is loss of potential talent!*

Intrapreneurship emerged as a revolutionary concept to improve the productivity and profitability of organizations looking for better ways to promote and retain talent. Leading companies across the globe adopted the concept for better productivity outcomes. Corporate giant IBM is one of the many organizations which encourage intrapreneurship within the organization.

The similarities established, it's now time to examine the things that set the two concepts apart from each other.

While the entrepreneurs have a whole lot of opportunities emerging from changes in their surrounding without any social or geographical confines, intrapreneurs are limited to the opportunities arising in the organization they work for. Most organizations' policies require intrapreneurs to seek permission before acting on their plan for the future. However, things are different in practice – intrapreneurs being the opportunists that they are, are more likely to act first and bear the consequences later.

One could term the intrapreneurs are the intra-organizational revolutionaries. They are out to bring change even if it requires challenging the system and fighting the status quo within the organization. This automatically leads to a moderate amount of friction which can be channeled positively for the greater good of the organization with mutual respect for each other in the workplace.

Intrapreneurship, however, does enjoy an advantage over entrepreneurship. Unlike the entrepreneur who has to make an effort to acquire the resources they need to accomplish their goals, intrapreneurs have the resources available within the organization at their disposal. These resources basically, make an intrapreneur's endeavor to exploit an opportunity easier than it is for the entrepreneur. Normally, an intrapreneur would look for possible slacks in the organization and designate them into their intrapreneurial ventures.

However, intrapreneurial innovation faces challenges of execution and recognition as organizations grow in size. There are several reasons that lead to these hindrances, including:

- When companies grow larger, it becomes difficult to ascertain who is doing what.

- Growing organizations tend to separate and specialize in their functions to help the business maintain greater focus, but the same leads to a rift in effective communication.

- Growing organizations promote increased competition. This to an extent may be healthy for the organization but in the longer run, employees tend to hoard their knowledge and skills instead of sharing them with others for the collective good of the company.

Intrapreneurship is entrepreneurship practiced in the corporate environment and it is important. Even organizations that didn't feel the need to adopt this concept are now contemplating the action; simply because they wish to be able to properly manage the talent pool available to them in the form of a millennial workforce.

Here are prominent reasons that essentially highlight the importance of intrapreneurship in the modern day corporate environment:

INNOVATION

To ensure top line growth in the market, organizations should be innovating all the time; and this does not mean an innovation initiative or two in a year's span. For sustained growth, organizations need to set up a proper framework of regular innovation. It needs to create the right environment for the right people working in the right processes to make the best of the situation. Intrapreneurship and innovation go hand in hand – one cannot work without the other and hence, intrapreneurship is as important as innovation for long-term growth of the company.

ENGAGEMENT

We have talked redundantly about engagement yes but bear with us. A research in 2012 by Gallup estimated that the US economy loses out on productivity worth between $450 billion and $550 billion annually because of actively disengaged employees.[25] We've previously discussed how low levels or absence of employees' engagement can lead an organization to retarded or no growth. Intrapreneurship creates opportunities for employees that are meaningful and challenging – resulting in a systematic forum for better employee engagement.

LEADERSHIP

Intrapreneurship propels the concept of leadership. It requires a special set of behaviors and competencies that can be employed to fully exploit the capabilities and skills of the executives in the workforce. Unlike conventional leaders/*managers*, intrapreneurs are driven by opportunities created by their work environments, using their aspirations and creativity to bring out the best from a situation. These are the people that lead the organization to better growth initiatives.

GROWTH

To be able to survive the cutthroat competition in modern markets, companies need to grow – and by growing we mean robust growth that allows them to survive and compete with their competitors. Intrapreneurship is all about implementing the entrepreneurial mindset within the confines of a given

[25] http://www.gallup.com/businessjournal/162953/tackle-employees-stagnating-engagement.aspx

organizational structure to create an innovative work culture and system that supports the overall growth of the business.

CHANGE

Organizations that resist change are often found reporting stunted growth. These organizations adopt a risk averse cultures that do not allow them to explore their complete potential. On the other hand, companies that are open to change are ones that are adopting new policies and strategies that help them boost their productivity, profitability, and growth. Intrapreneurs are always on the lookout for potential opportunities – opportunities that are created by environmental changes. They take risks and lead the way to bring the changes they wish to see in the organization.

Intrapreneurship, since its inception has grown into a phenomenon, a critical imperative that allows organizations to survive and grow better. The organizations which took the initiative to adopt this concept have shown remarkable results in the form of better innovation, increased productivity, improved employee engagement scores, and higher profitability.

But adopting the same concept for the millennials is not the same as for generations before them. The millennials work differently and hence, it is important to be familiar with the opportunities and challenges intrapreneurship brings for this generation of workforce.

Once an organization obtains the understanding of these challenges and opportunities, it can work towards formulating a policy that helps them exploit the full potential of this concept.

THE MILLENNIALS AND INTRAPRENEURSHIP –THE OPPORTUNITIES AND CHALLENGES

When the millennial workforce walks into the organization, they demand the company to change gears. Millennials are looking for work environments that are more flexible, creative, and far-sighted. Of course, innovation has been a constant part of most successful organizations for decades, but the new generation of employees is looking for some serious acceleration in the innovative pace of organizations when deciding whether the company they work for is worth staying in or not.

Combine all of the above mentioned demands of the millennials and it collectively shouts one word: Intrapreneurship!

As discussed earlier, the concept is the driving force behind structural, cultural, and environmental changes within an organization that help the business propel through the test of time. With the millennials who love doing things their way, intrapreneurship is a fantastic tool to assist them in improving the employee well-being, employee engagement, business lines, customer services, and more in addition to the core business of the company.

Let's take a detailed look at this.

THE MILLENNIALS AND THE INTRAPRENEURIAL OPPORTUNITIES

Unlike the generations before them, millennials aren't patient enough to wait through the cumbersome processes in conventional organization to create an impact with what they do.

They are rejecting the idea of putting in decade's worth of work to actually be able to have a say in the matters that are as important to them as they are to the organization.

Smart managers, instead of calling the millennials lazy and asinine would actually go an extra mile to comprehend the actual reason behind this inexplicable behavior. And there is a solid reason!

Although money is not everything for the Millennials, with the copious amounts of student loans most millennials are burdened with, it is no surprise that they want results and they want them now. Millennials have this trust of indulging meaningful work that creates a widespread positive impact on the field of their choosing in addition to the performance of their organization. They live for measurable results.

This thirst for creating an impact and finding meaning in what they do is what the organizations need to capitalize on. Instead of complaining about the lack of entrepreneurial thinking among employees, managers need to start closely observing the new generation of employees to pick out the ones that both think and act like business owners.

This is where intrapreneurship becomes a powerful tool for the management to properly utilize the complete potential of their millennial workforce. The phenomenon allows creative minds to explore the best possible ways to bring positive changes in the organization both internally and externally. Besides, the concept of intrapreneurship is not just limited to the core processes of the business. It could be implemented on everything from employee wellbeing to the launch of a new product, as long as it is reaping visible benefits to create an impact on the organization.

With the number of millennials in the workforce increasing day by day, a number of organizations are making paradigm shifts to openly embrace the idea of letting the millennials do things their way. However, the idea doesn't always pay off.

THE MILLENNIALS AND THE INTRAPRENEURIAL CHALLENGES

Now if you were to be told that you are free to do things your way – as you want and when you want – wouldn't that be something?

Having the freedom to plan, produce, and execute your work just the way you want can be exciting and challenging at the same time. It brings the thrill that millennials are looking for in their jobs – something that inspires them, motivates them, and engages them better. Intrapreneurship will give them all that, but it does not come easy.

The thing is that adopting an intrapreneurial approach to the work process will require a drastic cultural shift within the organizations. It will need a simultaneous change in the management and thinking patterns of the existing managers. Unless that is accomplished, intrapreneurship cannot possibly thrive in the organization.

For the most part, it is the internal resistance that leads to the failure of this fantastic talent management tool. These internal resistances can be in the form of:

THE CULTURE

The organizational culture is based on the way people within an organization, think and perceive different things. It's the mindsets of the management and the employees that have been accustomed to a certain way of thinking and working. Bringing about a cultural

change would mean changing the way people do their work, the way they approach a particular problem, the way they contemplate and look for viable solutions, or the way they determine the different aspects of performance.

While the millennials are relatively new in the corporate environment, their Generation X, and to some extent baby boomer bosses have been in the corporate world far longer. These generations have set ways of dealing with corporate matters that usually follow proper protocols – and it's not easy to change that. Millennials may be far more creative and better risk takers than the generations preceding them. Look around, they may not be registering businesses but they are doing business on the side (Selling products, marketing, etc.); but despite the organizations' willingness to grant them the liberty to do things their way, many organizations prefer sticking to their norms. This in turn limits the scope of intrapreneurial millennials to thrive and remain with the same organization for longer.

THE EXPECTATIONS

When millennials are granted free-will and autonomy they are burdened with the high expectations of the management and the other employees of the organization. While these expectations can be met over time, most organizations are driven by managements and processes aiming at short-term goals and results. This for the intrapreneurs is an added challenge.

Intrapreneurs are risk takers; their methods may be innovative, creative, and different from the conventional work styles, but they do carry the risk of failure. With the amount of attached expectations from others in the organization at stake, these intrapreneurs may be working in constant fear of trying not to fail – they'll play safe. Playing safe is a down slide for the initial concept of intrapreneurship, where the individuals are supposed to experiment, fail, and learn to find out what works best for the task at hand and the organization.

THE AUTONOMY

Innovation needs an autonomous environment to breed, but businesses are complex structures. This complexity is often displayed when defined processes limit the mobility of an idea or concept towards actualization. A simple example of the same can be seen in the response *"Your idea is great, but we are waiting for a go-ahead from the legal team to proceed with it."*

Operational and structural complexities within the business environment act as barriers for the free-flowing concept of innovation. Now if a millennial comes up with a stellar idea to bring down the operational costs of producing the new product, the idea will have to pass through different levels of management before it gets approved and implemented. This approval and implementation at that stage might be too late to create the desired impact. The purpose is lost and for the result-oriented millennials it's a setback in that might make them jump ships.

THE SUPPORT

Intrapreneurship is all about putting the right people in the right environment with the right opportunities and the right support to capitalize on the opportunity at hand. When we talk about support, it is not just the management and fellow employees but also the monetary funding required to ensure the conversion of an idea into quantifiable and measurable benefits.

For the most part, the millennials will have the support of fellow millennials in the organization, but most of them would lack the "say" in organizational matters that is needed to make sure the intrapreneur has the necessary freedom they need to lead, manage, and properly execute the project at hand while simultaneously living up to the expectations of the management. When this support is lacking, intrapreneurs have a difficult time scraping through the task.

THE FOCUS

Have you ever wondered the impact of *"That's how things work around here, we've always done it this way"* on someone who is trying to work in an alien idea into the system of the organization for the betterment of the organization itself?

We bet most of you haven't. But this is what mostly happens when the unconventional millennials bring new ideas and creativity to the way things are in an organization. The mere statement shuts doors on their face, it shatters their confidence, and make them lose focus.

The results? A disengaged millennial workforce and lower productivity.

It is important for organizations to be able to create an environment that can let the intrapreneurs breathe and flourish. Some of the organizations that find it difficult to bring cultural changes have resorted to separate intrapreneurial departments that have a working of their own and are encouraging intrapreneurs to progress and focus better.

Despite the challenges, intrapreurship is a human capital management tool too valuable to ignore. However, these challenges can be overcome by employing efficient strategies to foster a robust system of exploring, nurturing, and retaining millennial talent within the organization. We shall be discussing these strategies later in the book.

We cannot stress the fact enough that the millennials (even the most talented ones) are out in the corporate world with an agenda of their own. They'll flock to the opportunities that help them in achieving their goals without considering where or how they arise – these people, the bright talents are the most difficult to retain – and the organizations are in a fix over the effective management of this matter.

We're living in a world where technology has shortened the distances between the Eastern and Western global markets and essentially revolutionized the conventional way of working for most organizations. The economic transformation that followed has developed a set of challenges that is entirely new. These economic factors when combined with the demographic changes call for effective talent management tools and strategies to be employed by organizations to capitalize on the bright pool of talent they currently have at their disposal.

Facilitated talent mobility is just one of the strategic tools organizations can adopt to manage and retain the talent within the company.

That leads us to the inevitable question:

One may find several different definitions for talent management with a simple search on Google. However, most of them fail to properly explain the seemingly complex concept of talent mobility. By far, the most comprehensive definition for this talent management tool was given by *Lee Hecht Harrison* in their research report titled: *Mobilizing Your Workforce –*

Understand, Develop, and Deploy Talent for Success. The report defined talent mobility as:

"An integrated talent management process supporting talent movement that hinges on an organization's ability to effectively understand, develop and deploy talent in response to business needs."[26]

Primarily, the concept focuses on the mobility of talent within the organization, across roles, projects, teams, locations, divisions, and more in order to improve the overall score of employee engagement and employee retention. Talent mobility can be both, employer- driven or initiated by the employees. While the employer-driven workforce initiatives are called *"succession planning"* the employee initiated programs are called *"career planning".*

---

[26] Mobilizing Your Workforce – Understand, Develop, and Deploy Talent for Success 2015 (Page 4)

Before moving ahead, let's take a look at these key concepts first.

SUCCESSION PLANNING

Succession planning can be adequately described as the process through which an organization makes sure that its employees are hired and nurtures to take up each key position within the company.

With a proper succession planning process in action, you can recruit talented employees, develop their abilities, skills, and knowledge, and ready them for an impending promotion to roles that are far more challenging than the ones they are currently working in. When a company actively pursues a succession planning process, they are basically making sure that their employees are in a continuous process of professional development that prepares them for what lies ahead – career advancement.

You ask: *why is this important?*

When a company grows and expands its operations it is creating job opportunities and losing key employees at the same time. With proper succession planning, this loss of vital employees is adequately met with plausible candidates from within the organization who can fill in the place and resume the new roles without much difficulty – smooth transitioning and a cut in last minute hiring costs – because they have been developed for these roles.

CAREER PLANNING

Career planning is more of an individualized continuous process that involves several aspects. These could be different for each employee and may include:

- Identifying the values, preferences, and interests that inspire you

- Discovering the importance of life, learning, and work; and exploring the options available to you based on your skills and interests

- Making sure that the industry/profession you're in is suitable for your personal preferences and circumstances

- Adjusting your learning and work plans on a regular basis to align them with life changes or the changes in the workplace

There is no set time for career planning. It can be done by someone just out of high school or even someone who is sick of their bank job after a decade long banking career. Career planning is all about learning and developing as an individual and a professional; and it's continuous.

Regardless of what name they take, at the end of the day the success of the program largely depends on the willingness and actual mobility of an organization's talent within the enterprise.

Practically put, the concept of talent mobility is all about striking a balance between the skills, experience, and competencies that an employee is expected to deliver as a contribution to the organizational goals and the individual ambitions of these employees. It is about recognizing the talent available within the organization and capitalizing on it in the best way possible.

Businesses these days are implementing talent mobility programs to keep track of the internal movement of employees in the organization. However, what most of them don't realize is the fact that a talent mobility program done right has the strategic potential to yield significant results when it comes to business productivity, profitability, and growth. Our next topic will deal with the most prominent benefits of talent mobility in detail for better understanding of the concept and its importance.

HOW IS TALENT MANAGEMENT HELPING ORGANIZATIONS?

How do you identify a successful organization?

It's not just the one that has been reporting an increasing trend in profitability each

consecutive year. These profits may go down one of these years due to unforeseen event or an anomaly – *then what?* To identify successful organizations, one needs to observe the management that runs them.

Organizations where the managers/leaders are constantly trying to improve internal and external processes for better outcomes are the ones that move forward and attain sustainable growth. With leaders constantly striving for better results, the employees are automatically encouraged and pushed to follow suit with adequate opportunities being created for them to accomplish their career goals.

Now that we are talking about talent management in this book, this philosophy of a continuous effort to grow and improve can be consolidated in the concept of talent mobility. In order to get the most out of the existing employees in the organization, talent management alone doesn't work. It may ensure that the organization is hiring the best talent that is right for the position they're recruited for, but there is no guarantee that this very employee will remain focused and engaged in contributing to the accomplishment of organizational goals – hence, the talent mobility!

Talent mobility is what allows employees in the organization climb the hierarchical ladder and attain more challenging and influential positions that can help them make a difference to the organization.

We are listing down 4 key benefits organizations can enjoy after implementing a comprehensive talent mobility program.

IDENTIFYING THE RIGHT TALENT

We mentioned earlier that there is a war for talent going on in the modern day job market. With the situation intensifying every day, organizations are looking for lucrative solutions within their own walls. Sifting through existing employees to find the right talent brings forth three basic advantages.

1. It saves the time spent on external hiring.

2. It saves the additional costs of placing advertisement for vacancies and conducting robust hiring processes.

3. Existing employees are already familiar with and attuned to the mission and culture of the organization. They need less time to get affiliated with the requirements and expectations associated to their new posts.

There is another lesser known benefit of promoting existing employees to key roles within the organization instead of hiring externally. In 2015, the Human Capital Institute (HCI) conducted a research in collaboration with Oracle, which revealed that mobilizing talent within the organization resulted in better productivity. Almost 60% of employers shared the view that employees promoted to more challenging tasks often performed notably better than ones hired externally.[27]

A NEW GENERATION OF LEADERS

We are already aware of the fact that the Baby Boomers are nearing retirement, the Generation X is taking over their roles and there is a fresh influx of youngsters (millennials) in the workforce. *But who will take over once the Generation X decides to call it quits? Or what should the organizations that have a large majority of millennials in the workforce do to create leaders?*

The Global Human Capital Trends 2015 report compiled by Deloitte revealed that almost 53% of the millennial workforce is eager to assume leadership roles in organizations they work for, however there are only around 6% organizations that operate proper leadership programs for their employees.[28]

---

[27] https://www.shrm.org/ResourcesAndTools/hr-topics/talent-acquisition/Pages/Internal-Recruitment-Critical-Hiring-Retention.aspx

[28] http://www2.deloitte.com/content/dam/Deloitte/at/Documents/human-capital/hc-trends-2015.pdf

Through talent mobility organizations can create a strong leadership pipeline by focusing on the insight and vision required to identify the potential talent available within the organization. They can use parameters like learning capabilities, succession activities, and performance measures to assess the abilities of their employees and work on the best talent to develop them for roles that take them a notch higher in the organizational hierarchy.

REVOLUTIONIZING ORGANIZATION CULTURE AND INCREASING ENGAGEMENT

Our chapters on employee engagement and intrapreneurship laid adequate emphasis on the importance of active engagement and strong work culture for the talent retention and improved productivity. Most of the times, employee engagement strategies remain outwardly focused only on keeping the employees motivated – the practicality of employee retention runs far deeper than just that.

Mobilizing talent within the organization opens up doors for employees to face new challenges, buildup their skills and develop connections that help them achieve their career aspirations. It helps organizations create a culture that encourages each employee to bring their A-game forward in the hopes of meriting to the list of future leaders, hence automatically improving engagement.

A BROADENED SCOPE FOR THE HR

While in the past the Human Resource departments in organizations were limited to ensuring compliance and calculating benefits, their modern day functions have promoted them to the exalted position of a powerhouse trusted with the responsibility of managing talent.

When we say *'managing talent'*, we imply the development and implementation of strategies that allow the organization to attract, hire, train, mobilize, and retain the best talent within the organization. Creating talent pools that have the agility and ability to take the organization to new heights in terms of productivity and profitability does not come easy, and talent mobility is THE tool the HR needs to make it happen.

In his book *Good to Great*, Jim Collins succinctly describes the concept of talent mobility as:

"People are not your most critical assets, right people are! The ultimate throttle on a growth for any great company is not markets, technology, competition, or products. It is the ability to get and keep enough of the right people within the company."

It is hence no surprise that organizations with a clear vision of their core talent and critical positions possess a greater ability of mobilizing the right people to the right posts than those that don't. It gives them the ability to handle the most critical business related issues with relative ease.

Talent mobility may promote improvement in learning and contributions of the employees, but just like intrapreneurship this concept too is dependent on a proper structure, and this is where things get complicated – *not too much though!*

Over the years there has been a considerable increase in the number of companies that have been moving towards incorporating talent mobility into their talent management programs. The main cause behind this has been the challenges faced by organizations in acquiring and retaining potential talent that can be up-skilled to fill the roles of strong leaders in the future. By developing existing employees for the same, the talent managers are at least ensuring that they will have the new breed of leaders ready by the time the employees currently in the position are due for retirement.

Obviously, organizations are also considering the fact that internal mobility is relatively easier than involving in the detailed processes of external hiring – placing advertisements, short-listing candidates, conducting multiple interviews, and still not being sure if the best candidate is the RIGHT candidate for the job. Talent mobility is saving both time and money for organizations. Besides, it is working out as a fine alternative for financial motivation, which most millennials aren't always interested in.

So what's in it for the millennials?

Talent mobility is about employee empowerment. It is about developing the existing skills, abilities, and knowledge of the employees already in place to prepare them for the greater tasks ahead. Earlier, we discussed that the millennials are looking for jobs that are meaningful and help them as an individual to create an impact with what they do. They wish to have a 'say' in the matters of the organization. They do not want a normal 9-5 desk job where they clock-in, work the tasks assigned, clock-out, and leave only to come back and repeat the entire process again.

They wish to bring change and create a difference and talent mobility is giving them a chance to achieve all that. Maybe not immediately, but when working in an organization which has a robust talent mobility program, the millennials know that if not now, there will later come a time *(or maybe sooner than expected)* when they will be exactly where they want to be. This automatically makes them work for it, stay committed to their jobs, and improve with time employing innovation and efficient use of resources.

Do you see the concepts of active engagement and intrapreneurship at work there?

Where the concept of talent mobility brings numerous advantages to the company, there are certain limitations that undermine its effectiveness, and managers/leaders need to be aware of these.

LEARNING FLEXIBILITY

For the smooth flow of the process of talent mobility it is imperative that the existing employees of the organizations are open to learning and change. At times even the best talents are not comfortable in making a move from one position to another or accepting greater responsibilities of a new post. This can essentially stunt the overall effectiveness of the entire process.

When organizations engage internal mobility strategies, they are spending considerable time and money in developing their employees for new challenges. This pays off well if the employees are equally enthusiastic about better opportunities within the organization but falls flat if they are not looking for anything more than the monetary compensations. The example of Nebraska Furniture Mart (NFM)'s expansion into the Dallas, Texas market is a suitable one. The Berkshire Hathaway company conducted years of research and when they time came to fill positions and move people around, they held a very transparent campaign that allowed EVERY SINGLE employee to gauge their talent and ability in relation to the positions available in all of their existing and new markets. The result: a very smooth talent mobility and transfer across the organization.

FRESH TALENT

It may save the company a considerable amount of money to prefer internal talent mobility over hiring external talent, but it also deprives them from the diversification of their talent pool. When you hire new employees, they bring different experiences, skill sets, and approaches to the organizations. There is a good possibility that these new skills, experiences, and approaches help organizations mold their processes and policies for better efficiency.

It is a good way to introduce innovation and diversity into the business that can collectively contribute to the growth and success of an organization.

LACK OF PLANNING

No matter what business strategy or venture to take up, if it isn't properly planned it will fall flat. Similarly, the internal mobility strategy needs to be thoroughly thought out and effectively planned to minimize the fall outs that may be caused due to inefficient processes.

You need to make sure your internal mobility program focuses on candidates who actually deserve a spot among the future leaders. This will require you to closely scrutinize the performance, willingness, and suitability of each candidate for the roles available in the organization.

THE BUDGETS

Even though the functions of the HR departments within organizations are crucial for the overall improvement of the organization and its performance, these departments are given the least priority in budget allocations.

Spending on the training and development of employees is more of an investment. It can be capitalized when the employees are ready to assume the roles they are being prepared for. However, most organizations don't see spending on training, development, and nurturing of employees as a lucrative investment. Often times the HR departments are working on tight budgets and hence, fail to meet the expectations of the management.

This is one of the main reasons why the role of the HR department although vast in scope, still remains limited in terms of achievements.

If you're looking for proper implementation of the talent mobility concept within your organization, you need to make sure you take the steps necessary to avoid the setbacks that can result from these limitations and result in costs far greater than the return you reap from the process.

Dealing with millennials is all about establishing the organization's credibility as one that will help them create and capitalize on opportunities – the opportunities that can propel

their careers forward. And these opportunities are created with the active mobilization of human resources. Millennials are job hoppers and unless they're promised a chance to grow and excel at what they do, they probably wouldn't want to stay long.

Unfortunately, cumbersome processes and red-tape mechanisms do not promote a positive image of an organization among the millennial workforce. This result oriented generation is always on the lookout for organizations that understand and help them accomplish their career goals. While it may be the organization's top priority to retain the millennial talent they possess for a longer time span, they should always be prepared to let them go.

Your plans and talent management programs need to be built around the fact that at some point, *"the millennials will leave".* Thus every human capital management policy and strategy should be directed at ensuring quick-career advancements for the millennials. They wouldn't stick around otherwise – not even for the average 2 years' period.

Probably the most important thing to remember is that as different as the millennials may be from the generations preceding them, they will for a considerable period over the next decade be a part of a multigenerational workforce. Hence, as an organization you cannot center all your focus on promoting and retaining millennial talent. This leads us to the next topic of discussion: The concept of Individual Tailored Needs (ITN).

THE CONCEPT OF INDIVIDUAL TAILORED NEEDS (ITN)

When we talk about effective talent management, the concept is just not related to managing and retaining the millennial talent. Despite the recent influx of the millennials into the job market and the workforces, many organizations are working with multi-generational workforces. One may ask: *how does that affect the talent management process within an organization?*

The answer to this question is simple yet complex at the same time. For the most part, this book has discussed how and why organizations should focus on proper talent management for millennials – it's essentially what this book is about. In the real world, organizations are operating with an interesting mesh of three different generations. It's not just the millennials and we certainly don't want organizations losing out on their seasoned Gen X and Boomers only because they failed to take into account their interests when devising the company's talent management program.

Allow us to simplify this for you. You see, when we are looking at multigenerational workforces, one thing becomes quite apparent – they're all different. Maybe the Boomers and the Gen X may share quite a few professional traits, but the millennials come to work with their own set of expectations, and they DO NOT settle for anything less. This is something we have established previously in the book.

Now the biggest challenge faced by most human resource managements across the globe is to plan and devise talent management strategies that work across the board for employees, belonging to every generation within the workforce – it's like bringing the Boomers, the Gen X, and the millennials on the same page. *But has that worked?* Mostly not!

This is because; all three of these generations are different from each other. Where the Boomers are nearing a retirement, the millennials are entering the workforce, and the Gen X is preparing to replace the Boomers. All three generations are at a different career level and this is a major factor that impacts their behaviors and motivation. What might motivate the baby boomers to level up their engagement at this point might not work the same way for the Gen X. This is where the concept of individual tailored needs (ITN) comes into play.

As the name suggests, the concept revolves around the coining of plans and strategies that directly address the talent management requirements individually:

- For each generational group

- For each individual employee in the organization.

The concept can be looked at from the two different perspectives listed above. We shall be discussing each of these in detail. For properly understanding the impact of adopting Individual Tailored Needs for generational groups, it is imperative to first know how these generations work, what motivates them, and what puts them off.

Time and again we have been discussing the work style and attitude of the millennials. This time we are going to have a look at the two generations that preceded them, because without it our probe into the effective modern day talent management programs would remain incomplete.

Let's begin.

THE BABY BOOMERS

The baby boomers were born in post World War II era, falling between 1946 and 1964. This generation grew up in the relative ease and prosperity that followed the post war period. There are certain distinct traits that one can associate with them, like:

- The need to be valued – this is almost the same as the Millennials' need to be recognized and valued.

- They like holding a position of importance – where they are **needed**. They want to be a vital part of the organization they belong to, and they have worked their way to those positions.

- This suburban generation feels they are entitled to a good fortune. Again this is something you can find among the millennials too. The opinion that they *'deserve'* to be where they are and what they want to be.

- These employees demand respect and recognition in return for loyalty and engagement. You can expect them to disengage as soon as they feel they are not being adequately recognized and rewarded for their dedication and efforts.

- The baby boomers are generally optimistic. They flow with the hope that times will change and things will improve. However, unlike the millennials, the boomers may not be willing to take up the responsibility to actually work towards making things better.

For most organizations with a multigenerational workforce, the baby boomers are the senior most employees ideally stationed on the key managerial positions. When these employees are heading teams comprising of Gen X and Millennial employees, they tend to enforce their "way of working" on their subordinates.

"I'd like you to follow our previous stance on a similar project to make sure you don't go wrong on this one."

Or

"You've been told what to do, make sure you don't miss the deadline."

Now the Gen X employees may not find anything wrong with these commands, but look at them from a millennial's point of view and everything about it is just wrong. Because the millennials like to do things their way and they do not appreciate being told what to do and how to do it. This could lead to a possible rift. *How?*

Look at it this way; you're a baby boomer at a managerial position who demands respect. Your newest recruit, a millennial is brilliant at what they do, enthusiastic about starting their new job, and excited to share their innovative ideas to help the organization achieve its goals. This all may sound perfect, until you tell the millennia to follow protocol on a project and get approvals before taking even the slightest action.

You're using your legit authority – but the millennia doesn't approve of it. They rather go behind your back, do things their way. They override your decisions and that is disrespectful. But do the millennials care? No they don't.

Their intentions may not be to disrespect you, but at the end of the day they are doing just that and you don't like it. The actual problem here is not the clash of egos; it is rather the disparity between the basic approaches – You like to play it safe and the millennials are big on taking risks. *Now how do you two get along for the greater good of the organization?*

Read along, we'll be discussing all that later in the book; but first let's have a look at the Gen X employees and how they fit into this multigenerational workforce.

THE GEN X

The Gen X includes people born between late 1960s and early 1980s. Sometimes referred to as the Forgotten Generation, the Gen X has been overshadowed by the more dominant generations that came before and after them (the baby boomers and the millennials). *So what makes them different from the other two breeds of employees under observation?* To start:

- The Gen X employees aren't fond of the baby boomers – they don't trust them and their leadership. *Uh oh! More trouble for the baby boomer managers.*

- They are NOT at all optimistic like the baby boomers and believe what's meant to happen will happen – *is that a good thing?*

- They have a pessimistic attitude towards their work and are most likely to disengage at the faintest hint of being slighted. They feel their efforts and contributions are largely overlooked and ignored and hence, resort to withdrawing their interest in their jobs.

- They look to strike a balance between work and life; now there's nothing wrong about that – *but are they really successful in creating an optimum work-life balance?* The Gen X has been voiced the most dangerously disengaged part of the workforce and most of this could be attributed to the point we discussed before this one – they are skeptical and pessimistic.

- The baby boomers are not the only people Gen X has a problem with. They don't appreciate the millennials either. They find the millennials' *"we deserve this"* attitude cavalier and disturbing.

After reading all this about the Gen X, are we really sure that it's the millennials who are the 'trouble' generation?

When it comes to improving engagement scores for the company, the Gen X may pose to be the most challenging employees to engage. It's simply because somehow, somewhere, they themselves are unaware of what they want and what could help them overcome the barriers to better engagement.

They may have reservations against the baby boomers but they are all right with the corporate rules and protocols laid down for them. They do not have problems with following the system. *But how do you make them get past their grudges against the other two generations of employees?* You need to give them the room they need to explore and exploit their potential.

Another thing that organizations can do is to break down this facet of employees and treat them one individual at a time implementing the concept of Individual Tailored Needs. This will allow organizations to overcome the self-imposed barriers of the Gen X through properly recognizing and rewarding their efforts.

Effectively managing multigenerational workforces may present itself as a looming sword on Human Resources management departments across the globe. But it also brings a thorough set of advantages for the company. Besides, this challenge is not one that cannot be overcome with a little relaxation in rules and policies, a robust talent management program, and a strong human resource manager.

As mentioned earlier, we will be getting to these points later in the book, but before we do, there are other important matters related to multigenerational workforces that need to be discussed in detail.

The truth is that organizations have worked with multigenerational workforces for centuries. The only reason this dilemma has become more pronounced lately is the fact that modern day organizations face stringent competition in the markets and industries they operate in. This calls for the most efficient use of resources that reaps high value benefits in terms of low costs and greater revenues. And an organization cannot achieve this unless they have their employees working at maximum potential and giving in their best.

In the past, organizations weren't pushed too much by competition; but as the corporate world evolved and the number of industries and companies proliferated, organizations had no other option than making the most of what they had – and this included the employees. It was more of a 9 to 5 back then; but now it is about using every minute of every hour to contribute something meaningful to the organization and the accomplishment of its goals. *It never comes easy though!*

Stagnant retirements and the influx of millennials have increased the age difference in the workforces which may at one point or another has affected the personal connectivity among employees of the same organization. However not all of it is bad.

A multigenerational workforce brings an interesting blend of talents, ideas, experience, knowledge, and creativity. When you have employees aged between twenty-something and sixty-something, you are geared with absolutely anything and everything that you may require to excel as an organization. The only thing managers need to be careful about is to make sure they understand the perspective of each different age group and the things that drive them to excel.

At the end of the day, the mission is not to help these generations gel together; it is in fact gaining enough insight on them to devise strategies that can help the organization leverage the strengths of each group and harnessing them for the collective cause of accomplishing organizational goals.

Strategy is everything; building a wall or bringing everyone together to run a successful organization!

If you have ever lived in a home with parents and grandparents your first reaction to this would be:

"There's no way that can happen!"

And you could be right in your stance. These generations: the boomers, gen x, and the millennials are poles apart when it comes to ideologies, upbringings, and mindsets. Even belonging to the same family at times does not help them overcome these differences. But most of the times, when it comes to a common cause, the same people set their differences aside and work towards it. It's the cause that unites them.

Now, one could argue that they're *"family"*, and families tend to stick together come what may. The same cannot be said for an organization.

To an extent the argument is valid. However, the key element to focus on at this point is the *"common cause"*. Organizations that succeed are often ones who are on the same page with their employees when it comes to setting collective goals and targets. In order for organizations to excel they have to make sure their employees are working towards accomplishing individual targets that are aligned with the overall accomplishment of the organization's goals.

Organizations can help different generations at the workplace get along by identifying their individual needs and devising policies aimed at providing them with those. These may come in different forms: money, recognition, promotion, fringe benefits, better engagement, autonomy, authority or more. Your policies should be directed at making sure that your multigenerational employees set aside their differences and work as a family and strive to achieve the goals of the organization and their own in the process.

It is not entirely impossible as most would assume. Nebraska Furniture Mart, also largely known as "NFM" – one of Warren Buffet's Berkshire Hathaway subsidiary companies, successfully implemented a "Be One" policy encouraging all employees to focus on serving their internal/external customers as One (1) entity. That's the common goal executed with uniformity and consistency across all four retail sites. Management supported the initiative through empowerment. Guess what? *It worked!*

With the way human capital management is evolving lately, it wouldn't be long before organizations set aside these woes to optimize their productivity and performance.

At this point it is essential to work in the relationship between Individual Tailored Needs and individual employees into the discussion. This will help us understand the depth and relative importance of the concept in establishing a well-rounded talent management program.

INDIVIDUAL TALENT MANAGEMENT AND INDIVIDUAL EMPLOYEES

It may be easier to deal with employees in the form of groups – in this case their categorization according to the generation they belong to. While grouping employees on the basis of their generation can help organizations devise uniform set of strategies for each to effectively manage, motivate, and retain employees in each group, the same does not assure guaranteed success.

The first question to pop up in your mind would be: *"Why not?"*

Let's take an example. You are a manager in a company. Your department needs two new recruits to fill in junior positions. Your HR department manages to hire two of the best available talents in the market. One of them (A) had been previously working in the competitor's firm and the other (B) is just beginning their career. They are both millennials and they both enter the firm at the same level.

Your company has an effective talent management program in effect and both A and B are assessed and rewarded on the basis of a pre-decided set of policies that are designed to keep a consistent scale across the board for each millennial employee. According to your organization's talent management program, they both are the same – *but are they?*

A month after hiring them you seem to notice the stark differences that set them apart. Although A has more experience than B, he showed an engagement score lower than that of B.

You also notice that B takes key interest in their job, is more flexible towards the company's policies and plans to stick around with this job for a long time. A on the other hand is not impressed with the management and their rigid work styles, he isn't happy with the process of appraisals and assessments, he feels he isn't being adequately recognized and rewarded, and is also looking for a new job.

But weren't they both millennials? YES they were. So what makes them so different?

In a one on one session with B you find out that he is a young single father of a 3-year-old. He has a huge amount of student loan to pay off and a child to support. This is his first job after trying to secure one for the past 7 months. He is qualified and dedicated, and only needs a chance to prove his capabilities.

A on the other hand reveals that he has been working in this field for the past year and a half and hasn't stayed with the same company for more than eight months. He tells you that he likes his job but it's not as rewarding as he would like it to be. You also find out that A plans to fill in the senior position vacancy that just became available and he thinks he is a better candidate for it than B.

Two people belonging to the same generation but coming from different backgrounds and living in different circumstances – *do you think they will be motivated with or be driven by the same things?* That's an obvious NO. So even when you have a proper talent management program based on individual tailored needs for multigenerational workforces, you can't be sure it would work the way you want it to work.

While A would be motivated by a possible promotion and greater mobility, for B it may be the space he needs to explore his innovation and creativity to enhance the love for his job and excel at what he does. It is also obvious that since B plans to stay longer than A within the organization; it is B whose talent needs to be promoted and nurtured for succession planning.

This is where you as an organization need to distinguish between employees. Categorizing them according to the generation they belong to is a start, but once that is done you need to penetrate deeper into the backgrounds and circumstances that may impact the behavior of your employees. This is where you actually employ the concept of Individual Tailored Needs.

You design a one on one program for each of your employees to leverage on their strengths, and give them what they need to receive what you need in return. These employees could be from any of the three generations that constitute your workforce. You can't limit this concept to just the millennials. You need to consider the impact of this phenomenon on a broader spectrum.

In case you're curious about what the management can do to achieve optimum benefits of incorporating Individual Tailored Needs across the board for the entire multigenerational workforce and individual employees in that workforce, our next heading can provide you an insight.

EMPLOYING INDIVIDUAL TAILORED NEEDS (ITN) IN ORGANIZATIONS

Regardless of what industry you operate in, you will always have employees with diverse needs and motivators; and before moving ahead with the task of efficiently managing them, you need to make a conscious effort to gain an understanding of these needs and motivators.

Understanding these motivators and needs can be a difficult job. You can't just get to know them by simply looking at the employee of the class of employees under consideration. What you actually need to do is reach out to your employees and talk to them.

For the most part, this job should be undertaken by the personnel of the Human Resource departments within the organizations; or at least one should be present when the manager conducts these one-on-one sessions (not to be confused with performance review one-on-one) with the employees. When conducted properly, these sessions can reveal tons of information about the employee to the managers.

They can tell you where the employee is coming from, the circumstances they are in, the things they wish to achieve through this job, where they'd like to see themselves in the next two years, what they expect their salaries to be in the next appraisal, what according to them can improve the current culture of the organization, the hidden talents they possess, their likeness for their job, and a lot more.

Once you are familiar with what you need to improve engagement for your workers, here's what you need to do:

RECOGNITION AND REWARD

If you are currently operating on a one-size-fits-all program for rewards and recognitions, brace yourself for its failure. Like we previously discussed, there is a fat chance that the same set of rewards will not motivate all the generational groups and/or individuals, nor the uniform recognition program allow you to fairly assess different employees. *All employees are not made equal!*

You have to dig deeper. Get to know your employees. See what works for them and what makes you work. Take this knowledge and incorporate it into your program. Tailor your policies and strategies to cater each individual and /or generational group separately. This will allow you to respond to the needs of your employees in a better way, stimulate the formation of effective work teams, and adequately recognize and reward your employees for their efforts and contributions to the organization and its goals.

When each employee/generation is individually catered, the only competition that remains internally is the healthy sort. This is an active ingredient for building stronger teams within the organization. When employees know their needs and efforts will be recognized and effectively catered, they will be motivated to perform better on an individual basis.

LOOK FOR SHARED NEEDS

Now coming up with a different strategy for each employee can be a tedious job. Not just that, it will also eat up considerable time in figuring out what each and every individual needs to stay motivated and engaged. Here's a shortcut – focus on acknowledging the shared needs. There are certain things that everyone wants/needs, including:

- Transparency – no surprises. Communicate properly with all your employees; no surprises and timely feedback.

- Respect – everyone wants respect and deserves to be respected regardless of their age or career level.

- Learning – that's a given. Even you wouldn't want to stay at a place that makes you feel stagnant, where you're not learning anything new.

- Valued – When you work in a corporate environment, the worst thing that can happen to you is that you drown in the sea of employees without being recognized or feeling like you belong.

Make these elements a permanent part of your employee management program. This can help you provide the basics of employee motivation to each employee regardless of their position in the company, the generation they belong to, or their age. It will also help create an inviting culture for future employees and may be the sole reason current employees decide to stick with you longer.

As managers you need to take into account the fact that after reaching a certain level, it is not the money or benefits that motivate the employees. Other things like authority and respect is what they yearn for. This is especially true in case of the baby boomers and some of the Gen X employees in line for promotions. Therefore, it is imperative to make changes to your individual employee management plan as these employees progress in their careers and their individual goals change.

For this purpose, it is necessary for the management to conduct proper talk sessions with the employees to keep abreast their changing goals and requirements.

PROMOTE TEAMWORK

You've got three different generations working in your organization at the moment; why not make the best out of it? The boomers can boost the positive aspects of the organization with their optimism. The Gen X can keep things real for everyone in the organization with their skepticism; and the millennials can inspire change with their confidence, ideas, and enthusiasm. *That's a great employee mix right there!*

What you need to ensure is that each of these generations have the environment to freely practice these traits as they team up to accomplish the collective goals of the organization.

Build the organization's goals around a shared sense of responsibility and work that is powered by healthy skepticism, enthusiasm, and optimism. Bring them all together for the greater good – a shared objective.

At this point it is imperative for us to stress upon the leader and/or manager's responsibility to build trust among the employees and help engage better emotionally and professionally.

While it may seem ideal to manage talents based on their individual needs in order to let them flourish in their roles and make meaningful contributions to the organization – it obviously isn't that simple. We are obviously calling for a possible change in the organizational culture. See, the problem doesn't lie in implementing a new strategy – it is actually the proper execution that creates the most trouble for the organization. You've got to realize that a part of the employees within the organizations are on managerial positions

– yes, we mean the baby boomers.

Typically, the boomers have been in the organization longer than any other generation of employees; they are set in their ways and accustomed to a way of things at the workplace. Presently they are on the helm of the organization steering it towards its goals. Now one fine day, the human resource management within the organization decides they need to change the way they manage talent – *you think that'll be practical?*

Change, although inevitable is a slow process – it takes time for people to adjust to a new environment; and often it's the ones most set in their ways that find it most difficult to come to terms with the changes *(boomers again!);* but it's not just them. Apart from the millennials there is hardly any generation that is open and accepting towards change – you didn't really think the skeptical Gen X'ers would be okay with this absolute turnaround in the way the organization recognizes, assesses, nurtures, promotes, and rewards their talent.

So what should the organization do?

In order to make this substantial change, organizations need to take a systematic approach. Trial and error in a regular basis may disrupt the productivity and engagement of the employees. Therefore, organizations need to adopt a proper system that positively channels their efforts of improving the talent management of their employees. This brings us to our next topic of discussion: *the concept of integrated talent management.*

INDIVIDUAL TAILORED NEEDS (ITN) & INTEGRATED TALENT MANAGEMENT

With the evolving roles of the HR departments in modern organization, there has been a significant increase in the number and intensity of the challenges they face. They have to look beyond the obvious prerequisites of simplifying processes, streamlining them with the company's operations, and manage all this with the lowest possible costs. On the frontline however, the roles have switched to the more important task of gathering and developing a highly skilled workforce – through effective recognition, promotion, and retention of superior talent.

In short, the HR departments now play the pivotal role of creating a critical competitive advantage for the organization – *the ideal workforce!* And it all begins with a robust talent management program.

As the HRM, you may have managed to draw up the perfect talent management program based on individual tailored needs of your employees, but if you don't have the infrastructure to deliver it to those employees, you're basically back to square one. In order to hit the home run, you need to be able to hold the bat right and strike every ball pitched at you in the right direction.

What we mean to imply here is that a talent management program that cannot reach out to and bring the desired impact on the employees is only as good as one that doesn't exist. The concept of integrated talent management was introduced to deal with this problem. When managing several employees at different levels, based on their skills and talents, based on Their personal goals, based on their relevance to the organization, and more – even the best drawn policies can fall prey to the multiple complexities that arise in executing it properly.

Integrated talent management allows you to break down the complex components of your talent management program into simpler processes. This makes it easier for organizations to differentiate the talents available to them. These talents can then be assessed across the various core competencies like: talent acquisition, talent development, employee engagement, recognitions/rewards, and succession planning.

But the 'ease' alone is not the highlight of an integrated talent management system. It is in fact the merged technology that is re-shaping this aspect of the Human Resource Management. Integrated talent management software is an intelligent combination of strategy and technology that enables organizations to properly design and implement their talent management policies.

For the most part, integrated talent management software are designed to facilitate the talent strategy of the organization. Since no two organizations are same, it is rather impossible to have a basic program uniformly created for all organizations. These software are hence, custom made; tailored to support the business' unique strategy, tie up loose ends in the process, and transform the organization's talent management strategy into a comprehensive program that aids the grooming and development of new leaders.

WHAT IS THE INTEGRATED TALENT MANAGEMENT SYSTEM ALL ABOUT?

What we described above was only an overview of a proper integrated talent management system. In actual, these software are a lot more than just that. Essentially, an ideal integrated talent management system has four fundamentals. Almost every vendor in the market would offer the complete program suite for organizations – however, there are very few organizations that would or actually do realize the importance of the entire software suite.

In order to understand the complete impact and relevance of an integrated talent management system, it is imperative to dig deeper into its components and their workings. Here's what these are:

THE RECRUITMENT SOFTWARE

The first step for an effective talent management program is to acquire the best-suited talent for the organization. The recruitment software can help the HR personnel to get the top-notch talent in the door through adequate research, plausible sources, and effective channels of communication with the potential candidates.

These dynamic software make use of hi-tech innovations and platforms to provide the HR managers with talent acquisition tools that allow them to explore, discover, shortlist, and recruit the best available talent in the market. With the recruitment process made easier, organizations are granted the opportunity to enhance their talent pools and include talented employees to their workforce, who have the potential to bring the change they wish to implement.

THE LEARNING MANAGEMENT PROGRAM

As a next step, the talent management systems aim at nurturing the talent they acquired to help them gel into the new surroundings and excel in their current roles. Hence begins the learning process. Learning Management programs provide a common platform where the organization can administer courses, introduce training programs, and help employees improves their knowledge and skills collectively.

These learning programs can be tailored for each employee based on the skills they need to move up the ladder and/or perform better or could be used across the board to educate the entire workforce on the same matter. With this program in effect, companies can ensure their employees remain abreast with the latest in employee development in order to enhance their capabilities and improve their learning experiences.

THE PERFORMANCE MANAGEMENT SYSTEM

There could be several ways organizations can manage and keep track of their employees. However, when we are talking about the integration of the entire system, it is better to stick to one of the performance management software developed by programming companies to help organizations maintain a formal log for the performance of each employee.

Gone are the days when the managers used to sit down with their employees in an attempt to discuss their goals, strengths, and performance areas where they needed improvement. Today the process has evolved to a comprehensive program that leaves the assessment-based reviews behind and takes a more coaching-oriented approach to assess the progress of employees.

These programs allow organizations to widen the scope of performance assessments and include more people in the process to promote fairer and legitimate performance management. It is true that the technology is more or less shaking up the conventional performance review process, but as far as the organizations are concerned, most of it has been for the greater good.

THE COMPENSATION MANAGEMENT SYSTEM

Most organizations, usually the smaller ones but at times even the big ones manage their employee compensations using the Microsoft Excel spreadsheets. This might be a convenient way if you have a small number of employees and/or the compensation plans are extremely simple. However, once the organization begins to grow, the workforce increases. Similarly, when you begin employing and spending on new talent, your compensation plans become complex.

Looking at the scenario from the spreadsheets' point of view – these situations make the process cumbersome and difficult to manage. Compensation management software are designed to help organizations cut down on the manual labor and any chances of human error in compensation management. These modules automate the entire process which brings general visibility to it and makes sure the employees know the performance bonuses and other rewards added to their compensation. This even works as a great motivator.

Unfortunately, despite the availability of the complete set of integrated talent management solutions, most organizations do not consider investing in it a healthy prospect. What they don't realize is the fact that these programs are custom designed to provide the organization with its very own structure for proper talent management. An automated system allows businesses to integrate and optimize their talent management functions and strategies, which in turn can help them:

- Boost the morale of their employees

- Promote discretionary effort

- Improve overall productivity

- Reduce employee turnover

- Develop a culture for promoting innovation and creativity

- Gain from increased customer satisfaction

- Cost savings and better financial performance of the company

After reading all this one might be curious to know how integrated talent management alone can bring so much positive change within the company.

HOW IS INTEGRATED TALENT MANAGEMENT THE SOLUTION BUSINESSES NEED?

An integrated talent management system can help organizations overcome the drawbacks in their current talent management models – smart businesses are already making the switch. However, there are still many of them that do not understand why they need to jump ships from the conventional processes to the automated ones.

Perhaps the answer to that lies in the answer to the real question: *How exactly does an integrated talent management system help a business?*

Let's find out.

THE TECHNOLOGICAL SUPPORT

The first thing that pops up in favor of an automated talent management program is "technology". Even manual processes can be streamlined and improved continuously to achieve better outcomes, but the time consumed in doing so can be measured in terms of potential costs and overheads for the business. Automating the system will save time. It will cut down on the mundane, repetitive processes that slow down the entire procedure. It will help establish scalable interfaces that can be accessed across the organization to help people share important talent management data that pertains to them.

So basically, an integrated talent management program allows your company to grow and make the most of their human capital without wasting important resources like time and money.

INTEGRATED TALENT MANAGEMENT PROGRAMS ARE DESIGNED IN SYNC WITH THE CORPORATE STRATEGY

When we talk about fulfilling the human capital needs of an organization to put their strategy into working gear and achieve their targets, an integrated talent management system is what connects the dots between the two. A comprehensive workforce plan alone cannot work as long as it does not have an efficient talent management system backing its actual worth. This talent management system has to be aligned with the corporate strategy, and should look to transform the workforce plan into a reality. Workforce plans are what drive the integrated talent management system, and the process operates smoothly as long as the three elements are on the same page.

Together, the three elements lay out the answers to questions like:

- What talent is required to accomplish the short term goals of the company?

- Do we have all the talent we require? If not, how much do we need to acquire?

- How many new leaders would the company need in the next five years?

- Can we prepare the existing workforce to fill in these positions?

There could be a hundred more questions like these that basically highlight the human capital requirements of an organization in both the short and the long run.

THEY STICK TO THE STRATEGY

The fact that an organization needs a comprehensive talent management strategy in order to develop a robust talent management program is a no-brainer. You can't have a program without a plausible strategy. Integrated talent management software are designed to put that talent management strategy in action. The strategy is obviously designed keeping in mind the workforce plans of the organization.

Each activity/function of the integrated talent management program is formulated such that it achieves an objective of the strategy. If the strategy is weak, you can very much expect a low profile talent management system.

THE AUTOMATED PROCESS SHARES INPUTS AND OUTPUTS

We are all aware of the importance of transparency and two-way communication – it's something the millennials value too much *(had to bring them in here – been a while since we last discussed them)*, and since the book is primarily focused on the younger generation it is important not to miss out on something they might appreciate.

We are coming out of the sit-in-the-room talent discoveries and performance appraisals. Here's something that bring everything out in the open. Everyone knows the metrics used in their assessment, knows what training and learning opportunities are available to them, has a clear idea of where they are headed, and is aware of how their performance would be evaluated and rewarded. This transparency is something that motivates them into performing better and that obviously positively impacts the overall productivity of the company.

Besides, since all the processes that include: talent acquisition, succession planning, and learning and development; are streamlined, it is important for them to share information with each other. These processes will not be able to perform as well on their own as they can as a combined force. This is what makes the integrated talent management system an important component of the overall talent management process of the company.

IT SYNCHRONIZES THE ENTIRE PROCESS

Imagine a scenario: You are the part of an organization where each process of the talent management program is dealt with by separate HR personnel. Now the person dealing with the performance management is using a different model to assess your capabilities, and the one in charge of the succession planning is using one similar to the model used by the person dealing with talent acquisition.

So, which of the two assessment models is correct? The answer is both. *Which one would be used to judge your overall growth and performance for the year?* Now that's a tough one!

Using a different evaluation method at different processes can lead to contradiction and uncertainty in the outcome. There will seldom be a point where the two models would be able to deliver similar results. This glitch is eliminated when organizations implement the integrated talent management software.

The software uses the same language across the board. Whether it is yearend performance appraisal or an initial talent roundup at the hiring stage, all the data would be assessed, entered, and reported according to a preset metric.

HELPS CUSHION THE IMPACT OF DRASTIC CHANGES

Now this is an important one. We had been discussing the impact of cultural changes in the organization, and how not everyone is open to accepting change within the organization. Instead of announcing a full-fledged new policy on the changes in your talent management approach, organizations can soften the impact by implementing the infrastructure (the software) first, and gradually introducing the policies one by one as the previous ones begin to settle.

It will obviously be a gradual process, but at least you wouldn't have a host of angry employees refusing to actively engage in work because they feel the new appraisal policy is against their interests.

THE CHALLENGES OF IMPLEMENTING INTEGRATED TALENT MANAGEMENT

Just like any other policy or strategy, deciding to implement an integrated talent management program is difficult. It is not just software that you are integrating with the overall setup of your organization. It is a comprehensive solution to your talent management problems – the benefits we listed above are enough to convince almost anyone that this is what their organization needs to effectively deal with its human capital requirements. However, the process is not free from challenges.

The biggest challenge most organizations come across is coming up with an ideal software design. Like we mentioned before, in most cases these software are designed from scratch tailored according to the talent management program of the company, aligned to the long term talent management goals of the company.

Even if they do succeed in coming up with a design that adequately adheres to the aforementioned criteria, there is often the cliché of lack of simplicity, systematic approach, and practicality of the program – and that just brings the design back to zero.

Now what causes this?

Let's consider an example: You have a team of 15 HR personnel. You have tasked them to design the integrated talent management software plan. To make sure things do not get messed up, you divide the HR department into three different teams. One is told to design the talent acquisition function, the second is handed the responsibility for designing the learning and development program, and the third one is told to work on the succession planning software.

The way things are in the HR departments, these teams would immediately get to work. At the end of the prescribed time period, each team submits their proposed models for the processes assigned to them. They have all outdone themselves and the models look simple, practical, and even systematic. That makes you ecstatic.

However, the real problems arise when you have to combine these individual programs into one collective setup. These teams came up with brilliant designs for their individual jobs, but they forgot the bridges. They essentially missed out the important consideration that the program they design has to work in collaboration with the other two programs. Without these connecting bridges, the programs are nothing but an incomplete tool for the desired function.

The whole point of an integrated talent management system is to bring every single aspect of talent management on a single interface - a platform that can be accessed by everyone in the organization (of course with accesses limited as required). It is supposed to eliminate the inconvenience of a manual system, where the HR and the managers have to roam around the workspace calling in each employee one by one to assess their talent, evaluate their performance, and/or get to know what they want from their career.

We began this chapter with the aim to explain how individual tailored needs and integrated talent management come together to help an organization effectively manage and capitalize on the talent available to them within the organization. By now you have a clear idea of what these concepts are and how they work, but *what exactly is the connection between them?*

This takes us to yet another concept – the concept of skills inventory; and we'd be discussing all about it right about now!

WHAT IS SKILLS INVENTORY?

The skills inventory is probably the most significant connection between individual tailored needs and integrated talent management. However, before we move on to detailing this aspect of the discussion, it is important to first get an understanding of:

- What is a skills inventory?

- How does it work?

SKILLS AND PROFICIENCY

People often use the terms *"skill"* and *"proficiency"* interchangeably, *but are the two really synonymous?* The answer to that is: NO. Skills and proficiencies may be complementary terms but they aren't synonymous. Let's understand the difference!

SKILL

A skill is defined as a developed ability or aptitude for undertaking a particular task. It usually reflects the possession of specific talent and/or knowledge nurtured by education and experience. Skills are related to the nature of work a person does and the techniques and tools he makes use of in the process.

It is phenomenon that is vaguely described without a proper measure. A skill would be for example: Knowing French (language)

PROFICIENCY

Proficiency on the other hand is a measure of the degree of experience and knowledge a person possesses for the task they undertake. For example, on a scale of 1 to 10, how fluent are you in French?

So why are we discussing skills and proficiencies?

It's because the skills inventory requires precision to be effective. And skills alone cannot provide that. Hence, your skills inventory needs a pre-set measure of skill proficiency that can help you assess your talent better.

A skills inventory is basically a compilation of the education, experiences, and skills of all existing employees in an organization. Organizations that wish to implement integrated talent management software into their overall talent management program MUST prepare a skills inventory. How they manage to do that is contingent on the complexity and size of the business.

There are various ways to prepare a skills inventory; organizations make use of commercial software, database software, and sometimes even simple worksheets to pen down their skills inventory. But right now, it is not the method of preparation that we should be focusing on; because, regardless of how it is prepared, it will provide a correct summary of the organization's collective real-world experience, knowledge, and skills *only* if it's done right!

An up-to-date skills inventory can help the management identify existent gaps, if any, in the experience, knowledge and skills they already have and the experience, knowledge, and skills they require meeting the future goals of the business. The valuable assessments and information can then help managers take more informed decision in areas like:

- Recruiting candidates that are better able to fulfill the existing and future needs of the different business units.

- Appointing the right candidate to the right job – *that's what talent management is essentially all about!*

- Employing the best available talent to internal project teams for sustained success of the organization.

- Developing learning and training programs that are targeted to reduce the current skill gaps in the organization.

- Identifying the key players among the available talent that can be developed further for the future needs of the business.

- Creating an internal talent mobility channel that can enable the replacement of key managers and employees as and when they leave the organization.

- Developing a comprehensive workforce plan that is based on the strategic future needs of the business.

Going through the areas that can be influenced by a skills inventory, there's not an inch of doubt remaining about the fact that skills inventory is an imperative tool for effective talent management within an organization. What is important to note at this point is that preparing a skills plan alone doesn't work – this plan requires regular maintenance.

As the usual process of staffing, attrition, and training and development continues, there is a subsequent change over time in the knowledge, experience, and skills of each employee. The concerned managers need to be on their toes with the skills inventory maintenance, updating it regularly through a proper process. Since the skills inventory is supposed to provide with a clear picture of the talent in an organization at a particular time period, a stagnant inventory of skills will eventually lose its credibility if it is not updated on a regular basis.

Simply put, a skills inventory is a potent tool for the managers to improve their decision making for better management of talent. The skills inventory in addition to helping managers take better decisions assists them in identifying the individual needs of their employees and how those needs can be leveraged to bring out the best of them.

In other words, the workforce plan we repeatedly talked about when discussing integrated talent management, can only be drawn properly if managers take into account the skills inventory and the individual needs of their workforce that should be addressed through integrated talent management software.

Still don't see the connection?

Let's take an example. So your organization is planning to implement robust integrated talent management software to support its already functional talent management program. Since the integrated talent management software are generally made to order, the vendor you approach asks you for a workforce plan.

You then set out to prepare a workforce plan. Now the workforce plan usually has two different aspects: the operational plan and the strategic plan and it's a detailed process; certainly one that cannot be achieved overnight. Workforce planning is the process of systematically identifying and analyzing the quality, type, and size of workforce that an organization would need to accomplish its long-term and short-term objectives. It sets the parameters of the mix of knowledge, skills, and experience that the organization needs and the steps it needs to follow to get the right people in the right number at the right place and time.

You realize that this might take longer than planned, before a sane voice in the team mentions the skills inventory. You've been working on one since the beginning of your talent management program and have been meticulous about keeping it up-to-date. That's half of your work for preparing a workforce plan done right there. The skills inventory gives you all the skills, knowledge, and experience the organization collectively possesses at this point; it even highlights the skill gap that needs to be bridged and the only thing left now is to see what needs to be done for the future.

So you draw up the workforce plan and head to the vendor again. This time they set to design your program based on the overall talent management program and workforce plan you just submitted. However, once they reach the stage where they have to develop the learning and development and succession planning software, they again turn to you in anticipation of your strategies. Only this time, they just want you to define the succession planning and training approach you wish to act upon with your integrated talent management.

For this purpose, you need to implement the concept of individually tailored needs to make sure the comprehensive design of your integrated talent management software is one that caters to the individual professional and personal career related aspirations of all your employees.

We hope the concept is now far better embedded in your minds than it was before. Talking about something as valuable as the skills inventory, it would be a shame to wrap the entire topic up in just a few paragraphs. The reason why this tool holds an esteemed position in talent management is because apart from assisting decision making, it has been found effective for the strategic planning process of the business as well. Let's get a better insight into what that means.

The core department responsible for the effective functioning of the talent management program is none other than the Human Resource itself. Their decisions and planning directly and/or indirectly contribute to the success or failure of an organization. They have the responsibility to identify and analyze the need for availability of the right human capital in order to achieve the goals and objectives of the organization. In addition to that, the Human Resource management is also responsible for preparing and maintaining a comprehensive skills inventory that can help them in various ways.

A well-crafted skills inventory contains information that in addition to carrying details of the employees' current jobs, includes enough data on the employees that can provide recruiters with a heads up on who is capable of what, and even keep an eye on the development of key employees who are qualified enough for any other vacancies arising within the organization. It provides a point of quick reference and evaluation to the HR management and helps them assess the employees' skill sets better. But when we talk about strategic decisions, it is more about understanding the current talent and what needs to be done to upgrade them for the future skill requirements of the organization that can help it achieve its goals.

Strategic planning aspects may include:

RECRUITING

Skills inventory adequately tracks the skills and progress of the employees currently working in the organization. This allows the human resource managers to focus more of their time on recruiting the right people for the right job at the right time. *How?*

LEARNING & DEVELOPMENT VS TRAINING

Another set of terms that are often confused to mean the same are *"training"* and *"learning and development"*. Prima facie, they both implicate the same outcome: employee development, but there is still one thing that sets them apart.

LEARNING & DEVELOPMENT

The systematic process of learning and development is imposed upon the employees to prepare them for future responsibilities and leadership prospects. Learning is about self-development; It includes acquiring knowledge or additional skills that can help employees contribute better to the organizational goals.

Learning and development is based upon the concept of "educating through experience"

TRAINING

Training takes a systematic approach to improve the skills, knowledge, and work attitudes of the employees with the aim to sharpen their abilities. The aim is to gear them better to excel at their current responsibilities.

Training is often imparted by an experienced facilitator or instructor, who has the relevant knowledge and expertise on the subject of the training.

By summarizing the skills, knowledge, and experience currently available in the organization, the skills inventory sufficiently highlights the "skills gap" that needs to be bridged for the organization to achieve its goals. This gap once identified can guide the human resource managers into taking the right hiring decisions

– decisions that will make sure the organization has the necessary manpower to drive it to the accomplishment of its short-term and long-term objectives.

TRAINING

One of the most important functions of the human resource management is to make sure they create ample training and learning opportunities for the employees within the organization. Employees, regardless of what generation they belong to have a thirst for growth. The only way they can ensure sustained growth is by acquiring new skills, making continuous improvements, gaining relevant experience, and enhancing their knowledge – without all this, the employee becomes stagnant *(something the millennials dread big time!).* So it would be safe to assume that employee growth is directly proportional to their learning and employee growth is eventually responsible for bringing overall growth of the organization.

Now that we've set the grounds for the importance of learning and training programs for employees, let's connect it to the skills inventory. Since the skills inventory identifies the gap between the skills an organization possess and the skills it needs; the human resource management can easily deduce learning and development and training programs it must initiate to upgrade the skills of existing employees to the level where this skill gap can be closed. It will also help them make other informed strategic decisions related to the urgency of the matter and the budget required to achieve it.

SUCCESSION PLANNING

Another HR function, and an essential tool for proper talent management is: Succession Planning. It provides Human Resource managers the far sightedness they need to draw up a talent management program that is providing legit successor to key positions in the organization in addition to acquiring, nurturing, and retaining the top-notch talent in the organization.

It is obviously impossible to include every single employee in the succession planning program, especially in large organizations. This is why succession planning is always focused on the cream of talent present in the organizations – one just can't deny that some employees are better than the others. It is these employees that with the adequate training, learning and development can be geared up to fill in for leadership positions when they get vacant. The challenge here is identifying the employees that are worth investing in – we say "investing" because the organization would be spending considerable time and money on them to bring them up to the level where they are ready to take charge.

This is where the skills inventory comes into play. Because you have all the collective skills, experience, and knowledge of your employees compiled at a single place (a spreadsheet, a database, or a program) you can simply pick out the best talent to take forward.

Let's take an example.

Employees A and B are new recruits in your organization. They both have the same skill set and the same level of experience in their line of work. *How do you decide who to invest in for the department's succession plan?* You decide to put them both through a series of challenging tasks. At the end of the process, you discover that even with the same level of experience and skills, B is more proficient in his tasks than A.

Now how do you find that out? Remember that *"Skills and Proficiency"* segment in the beginning? A skills inventory is of no use unless it has a precise representation of the skills currently present in the organization. What makes the skills measurable and precise is the level of proficiency. Your Skills inventory highlights that B is more likely to be a better candidate for the succession planning, because he has the efficiency and expertise that can be further polished to bring out relevant leadership qualities in him.

This helps HR managers design and plan appropriate career plans for the intended successors, and also makes sure there is little or no wastage of resources in the process. It also ensures that the right strategic decisions are taken to align the succession planning of these 'gifted' employees with the overall progress of the business itself.

PROFESSIONAL ALERT

Very often, especially in companies that have a high employee turnover, it is difficult to keep track of the talent movement. With people joining and leaving all the time, it is not easy to keep track of what talent still remains within the company. This is obviously a case of organizations that have a majority of their workforce comprising of the millennial generation.

However, this is not the only reason. At times the issue can be attributed to the laidback attitude of the Human Resource managers. It is the duty of the Human Resource department to keep a track on the recruitments, resignations, and dismissals taking place in the organizations. Human Resource Departments that fail to stay on top of this issue often lead their organizations into a dreaded corporate downfall.

One might think that "corporate downfall" is a harsh term; but look at it this way. The current war between industry competitors is all about snatching the top most talent of the industry and making sure it stays with them. In case of the above mentioned organizations they might be able to recruit the best talent but they are obviously failing at retaining them. Not just that these organizations are having a tough time keeping track of the talent coming in and going out of the organization. *Do you think they could ever win at the talent war?* It's an obvious no.

There are other types of organizations that do not face a talent drain but are having trouble managing their talent properly simply because they are unaware of the skills, knowledge, experience, and potential their employees possess that can be capitalized on to get the best out of them.

These are two different organizations but the problem they face is more or less the same. They do not know what human capital they have at hand and how to exploit it.

The solution? A skills inventory!

When you maintain a skills inventory, the very first requirement you need to fulfill is the commitment to keep it updated. It compiles all the talent an organization has at a certain time period and is regularly maintained to keep up with the changes in the workforce. Whether it is a case of high employee turnover or the lack of awareness, a skills inventory can work as a professional pointer that allows human resource managements to timely identify new talent and plan their careers accordingly in line with the growth of the business.

If you take the time to notice, we started off this book with the curious case of talent management and how it can help organizations manage and retain the millennial talent within the organization. But as we dug deeper into the concepts and drivers of effective talent management, it has become increasingly apparent that the problem is not just limited to the management of millennial talent. It extends far greater than that.

With most modern organizations working with multigenerational workforces, to concentrate all the attention on making the work culture and environment welcoming and rewarding only for the millennials can instigate an uprising within the organization. You may be able to pacify the outspoken millennials with talent management programs designed to facilitate their career growth but the skeptic Gen X'ers may feel left out and resist the change – it would be the employees against the system. *Obviously none of us wants that.*

What organizations actually need is a comprehensive talent management program that does not only address the concerns of the millennials – of course they remain the main focus of the program but without neglecting the other employees belonging to the other two generations. This calls for strategies.

Time and again we have been stressing upon the need for effective strategies, making use of appropriate tools and techniques to motivate, drive, and develop employees for the collective benefit of the organization and its employees. If there is anything that determines the success or failure of a mission (a business, a policy, a game, or anything else) it is the strategies used for them. Even the best business plans and ideas fail because the strategies behind running and sustaining them fall flat.

It is the strategy that will help you design a robust talent management program. It is the strategy that will put it into effect. You will need a strategy to make sure the talent management program is going according to plan and a strategy to make sure any fallout can be efficiently dealt with. At every step of the process, you will be required to come up with the right policy and tactics to see the program deliver the results you desire from it. And trust us when we say that the strategy is the toughest part of the entire process.

Over the course of the next section, we will be discussing strategies. We know the problem; it is now time to take a look at the possible solutions to overcome it. Every concept that we have discussed over the course of this book will be revisited, but this time with a different point of view. This time we will be looking at the ways in which managers can make the system better in order to inspire and motivate their employees and making the most of the human capital available to them.

At this point, we feel it is important to note that dealing with the millennial crisis WILL bring a drastic change in the culture of the organization. While the millennials may not have any difficulty adapting to it, the other generations may be faced with the monumental task of getting familiar with the new setup and adjusting their ways according to it. Your priority at this stage is to soften the blow as much as you can.

SECTION 4: HANDLING MILLENNIAL CRISES - HUMAN RESOURCE MANAGEMENT STRATEGIES

Today, probably the biggest challenge faced by organizations is: competition. There's a fierce competition out in the market for greater market shares and better innovation. There's an ongoing price war and the never ending efforts to achieve cost effectiveness.

Then there's the undeniable competition in the industries for "talent". It is talent we're all after; and why not! It's the right talent that can drive the organization to where it wants to reach. However, problems arise when it comes to attracting, hiring, and retaining the right talent. Modern day hiring processes are obviously more focused on the millennials – it's them who are entering the job market at this point. They are talented, educated, and most importantly enthusiastic.

What most businesses fail at when it comes to hiring and retaining millennial talent is keeping their enthusiasm alive. Boredom is the killer of creativity and a monotonous work environment with little or no challenging aspects to it is nothing more than – *boring!* The millennials like to be on their toes. They like responsibility. They appreciate learning and subsequent growth. They are out to chase their dreams and hence it is self-actualization that matters to them more than anything else in their career.

The Maslow's Hierarchy of Needs Pyramid

SELF ACTUALIZATION

According to the Maslow's hierarchy of needs, a person's needs are divided into five different levels. The most basic being the physiological needs, flowed by the need for safety, love and belonging, esteem, and self-actualization at the top of the pyramid.

WHAT IS SELF ACTUALIZATION?

Simply put, self-actualization refers to the need of utilizing one's complete creative and analytical potential to achieve greatness in what they do or wish to do. Self-actualization is as Kurt Goldstein put it:

"What a man can be, he must be."

Self-actualization cannot be accomplished unless one has the freedom and the commitment required to make the most of their skills, talent, knowledge, and expertise to reach a point where their desire of self-fulfillment is achieved. Like we mentioned before, the millennials are driven by their dreams and they have the motivation and commitment required to chase and fulfill those dreams.

However, somewhere after they enter the professional world, this enthusiasm is lost – it is killed. They, in most cases do not have the environment that allows them to flourish and grow as professionals. *The results?* They switch jobs. So, even if you successfully manage to recruit the top notch talent in the industry, if you do not provide them with a work culture that helps them to fully explore and employ their talents – the very thing you hired them for – there's little doubt that the millennials will not stick around with your organization

for a long time.

And that's where the problem lies!

Saying that this alone is the problem may not be the real picture. We mentioned in the previous section that the millennials alone should not be your only concern when it comes to devising policies for efficient management of talent. Being an organization with a multigenerational workforce, you've got to pay attention to the needs of the other employees too – specifically the Gen X.

So what do you do? You look for the right strategies and prioritize the things in order of their importance; and it all begins with identifying the need of the hour.

IDENTIFYING THE NEED OF THE HOUR

The need of the hour in most specific terms is: to implement a talent management strategy that brings the multigenerational workforce at the same wavelength. Of course, the focus would be slightly greater on the millennials, but you have to be on your toes to make sure you keep the boomers and the Gen X'ers adequately engaged for the optimal use of your skills inventory.

What we're looking for at this point is the establishment of a flexible work environment. One that allows the employees enough space to learn and grow – achieve self actualization to be precise. All this calls for a strategy. You need a strategy that will pull everyone together as one, yet give them the liberty to prosper individuality.

This strategy needs to focus on three core areas. There will be a lot more adding to them over time, but for a start limit yourself to improve on the following.

THE COMMUNICATION

We are looking for a one-in-all solution for the workforce issues organizations are facing in managing talent. Effective communication forms the backbone of a successful organization. Conventionally, the flow of communication has been more inclined towards the top-to- bottom communication style. The managers issue orders and the subordinates oblige. The older generations may be ok with that, but the younger generation is definitely not taking it well.

It's not just about the younger generation; effective communication is possible only when the information flows both ways. There has to be a clear message delivered with the expectation of a feedback. Millennials are big on feedback. They like to express their opinions; they have been brought up to voice out what they think, and they expect a feedback in return too.

The boomers today are managers, with the Gen X filling the senior subordinate positions and the millennials being hired at the junior positions. There is a vast difference in the way these three generations communicate. While the baby boomers and the Generation X have been accustomed to a more formal approach in written and oral communications, the millennials like everything else have a casual attitude towards communication.

Where the Ger X'ers would prefer emails and phone calls, the fast-paced millennials will resort to instant messaging or texts in addition to an informal language and tons of abbreviations. This could lead to a possible gap in the communication and also a perceived *"lack of respect"*. Communication has to be two-way to see that the information has been received by the intended listener, understood, and acted upon.

Like we said you have to set your priorities, effective communication is definitely one. There is no point in making three different generations work together towards a common objective if they cannot and are not able to communicate properly with each other.

THE UNCONSTRUCTIVE STEREOTYPES

"This is how things go around here."

This single sentence has sent the creativity, ability, and the desire for change of many to the deathbed. It is discouraging in addition to being clearly unnecessary. Many would argue that it maintains uniformity in the work process or saves them from unexpected workplace disasters; that most traditional policies/processes have been tried and tested for years to anticipate their results and then implemented in the organization to ensure the desired outcome.

But they forget something very important: CHANGE.

The corporate world is rapidly changing and so is everything in it. The processes that used to seem feasible a decade back is now proving impractical and unreasonable. The previous generation may have been able to get away with the infamous *"This is how things go around here"* but look where it landed the Gen X'ers. It killed their creativity and made them unenthusiastic and skeptic. They still find it difficult to accept the baby boomers and their ways of working so their best defense for it is pessimism.

However, unlike the gen X'ers the millennials are not giving in. They are rejecting stereotypes and making sure they do not settle for something they do not agree with – *precisely why you find them hopping jobs frequently.*

Overcoming stereotypes is difficult. The 'oldies' are mostly set in their ways and have been so for a very long time. When you attempt to break stereotypes there would hardly be a scenario where you're not faced with strong opposition. At some point it might even be you who has to change their ways to make sure everyone in the organization gets along properly.

No matter what you do, change is inevitable. You'll *(managers)* have to change some, they'll *(workforce)* have to change some. Again it has to work both ways. One can't expect a particular group of people alone to make the change. It has to be an initiative from both sides. Also you need to keep in mind that breaking stereotypes is not an overnight feat. It will require patience and effort on everyone's part to come to terms with things that are new to them.

Stereotypes are barriers to progress. This alone is a reason big enough to place it on your priority list.

Since we were talking about taking a step away from the norms, this is a good time to discuss how cultural expectations of different generations secure a place on the priority list. For that you need to understand how the work psyche of all three of these generations has been conditioned.

For the baby boomers it is the brick-and-mortar philosophy. For as long as they are on their desks, they are "working"! This means showing up for work at 9 am sharp and working after hours to show their commitment to their job. The Gen X grew up with both their parents striving hard to make ends meet. They saw them sacrificing personal/family time for the sake of work and hence this generation believes in striking a balance between work and personal life. Millennials on the other hand, grew up at the time of the great economic upheaval. They saw their parents losing jobs despite being loyal and committed to it, therefore this generation is all about focusing on the life outside the work environment.

Each of these generations brings a different set of work culture expectations to the table. Often organizations find it difficult to address these expectations in a way that they satisfy the employees without disrupting the overall work environment. The easiest way about it is obviously introducing greater flexibility in the work environment and allowing each generation to pursue their individual work style – one they consider best for them.

The biggest opposition to this theory is that if allowed, there would be no uniformity in the organization's work process. But look at it this way; wouldn't you prefer a flexible organization that gets along and works together to achieve the common goals over one that has a set pattern of work style and finds it difficult to overcome the challenges of multigenerational workforces?

Think about it.

The first step to address a problem is to identify the root cause behind it. Once you are able to accomplish that, everything else starts falling into place. From the beginning of the book we have been discussing the problem:

"The effective talent management of millennials"

But the problem is unfortunately far deeper embedded than just that. Truth is, most organizations are not willing to make the change. They think it's too much of an effort and find a convenient target to put the blame on – the millennials. What they are continuously missing out on is the fact that it is impossible for the company to move ahead on the road to success without adapting the latest requirements of the changing corporate environment.

You have to begin somewhere, and the best way about it is to bring your multigenerational workforce on the same page. The three priorities we discussed above can help you set up a work environment that allows all your employees to settle and get along well. We will be talking about how you can achieve these priority goals before moving on to the talent management solutions that can help you get the most out of your millennial workforce in the following chapter.

As we explore further into the plausible solutions to manage these problems you will notice that most of them demand the organization to make substantial changes to their work culture. This is what this book is about. However, it wouldn't be fair to give the entire credit of this "required change" to the millennials alone. Yes, they may be nothing like their predecessors and may be out to reject the well-accepted norms of the corporate culture but it's definitely not just them for whom the culture needs to be altered.

The problem extends further than that. It is actually the *"need of the hour"*. The chapters that follow here forth are only going to help organizations that are willing and committed to make the change. The ones that can put the long discussed phenomena of curriculum, discipline, and stereotypes aside to accept the ones that can actually bring about the difference they wish for.

It's time to change. Time to bring some chaos to the workplace, trigger the creativity, and let the talent flourish – there's a plan right there. To make sure this plan sees its due execution, you need working strategies to manage the talent available in the organization to its complete potential. The next chapter is all about strategies, the ways you can bring around the best of talents together to achieve the goals you've set for the organization as a whole.

Without further ado, let's get down to business.

We established in the previous chapter that organizations need to upgrade their talent management activities in order to achieve the complete potential of the business. In the earlier sections of this book, we discussed a series of different talent management tools that organizations can collectively or individually implement to obtain their desired results.

What's interesting to note here is that even with all these tools and techniques being highly effective in their own capacity, they may not work the same way for every organization. Each organization has different dynamics. They have different structures, different priorities, different goals, and different management styles. Since talent management begins from the drafting of a comprehensive workforce plan, every organization has its own workforce requirements that decide the course of its talent management program.

It requires a particular strategic plan catering strictly to the needs of that organization in particular and includes goal alignment to ensure maximum productivity and profitability. Strategic plans make sure that everyone in the organization is on the same page and moving steadily towards the accomplishment of common goals in addition to their individual goals. Different strategic plans call for different working strategies to achieve results.

Hence, the talent management upgrade for every organization has to be designed in accordance with their specific plans for organizational growth and the talent required for achieving this growth. The strategies we will be discussing in the upcoming chapters are generally applicable across the board.

What you have to do is understand each and assess them in relation to your organization's specific work environment. Ask yourself questions like:

- Is this what the organization needs?

- How will this strategy help us promote and retain good talent?

- What is the opportunity cost of implementing this strategy?

- Can there be a better alternative for this given our situation?

- Will the strategy work well with our present system?

- How much would it cost us to implement the strategy?

- What would it take to ensure the proper functioning and effectiveness of the strategy?

There will be instances where everything about the strategy is working in your favor; at others the opportunity cost of implementing the strategy may be too great to consider it feasible. You have to look for strategies that give you the most benefits for the least possible costs.

We'll be, one by one, discussing the strategies to make the concepts of Active People/Employee Engagement (APE), encouraged intrapreneurship, talent mobility, and individual tailored needs more effective and fruitful for the organization. Read through them and pick the ones that you feel will help your organization prosper.

Here's a quick refresher: *Active People/Employee Engagement (APE) is the name given to the process whereby companies can ensure that each of their employees is completely involved in and passionate about their work.*

We know what employee engagement is and how it can help the organization. Right now, it is time to learn how as an organization you can work towards improving the engagement level of your people/employees. In order to have the employees invest the best of their hearts, minds, and hands, organization leaders can explore the following avenues of action

– we call them the four (4) principles of Active People Engagement.

TEAMWORK

Teamwork in an organization is like a well-lubricated machine that ensures the timely completion of projects and jobs. Obviously, a team needs a leader for functioning properly – a leader that connects with them on both professional and personal levels.

A successful leader is able to connect with their employees. It is about showing and making the employees realize that they are valued by the management. Experts often argued that it is employee-focused initiatives like work-life balance and profit-sharing that can help employees engage better, but they tend to miss out the positive impact a healthy employee-manager relationship can have on the quality and quantity of work submitted by the employee.

A fractured relationship between the manager and his employees can undo any positive impact of any employee-focused initiatives implemented. A greater part of employee engagement reflects what employees feel about their relationship with their bosses. An employee is the most valuable asset for an organization and companies that acknowledge this fact and make their employees feel valued are the ones that have the best scores of employee engagement.

Listening forms the core of active engagement. Employees just like everyone else have the need to be heard and seen as individuals. When employees are given a chance to speak they feel valued and put in effort to reciprocate the gesture with outright commitment and dedication to their job.

We've all heard about the multi-industry giant "Virgin". The organization has one of the most successful employee engagement scores and they owe this success to their policy of listening to their employees. The organization understands the importance of making their employees feel valued. They listen to the opinions of their employees and make an effort to understand their perspective on different aspects of the business. They conduct debates and promote employee ideas that help their employees grow and realize their worth for the organization.

When you listen to each individual in the team, it gives you the opportunity to get a better insight into the things that inspire and motivate them. While some may be looking for better appraisals, others may just be after getting to spend more quality time with loved ones (work-life balance). When you let the employees express themselves and the way they'd like things to be, you make them a part of the decision making process. This promotes trust between the two parties, reduces the employee stress levels, and even establishes a culture where employees own their problems and look for plausible solutions for them.

Teamwork is not possible without effective team building. A team is a structure that brings employees and management together as they strive to achieve common objectives. There is therefore, a need to establish strong collaboration between the members of the team – and it all begins with the managers/leaders. It is you – the manger – who has to be the glue that binds the team together. You have to promote a culture of active discussions and debates, bring employees of different calibers together and gel them into a single unit.

These members of the team that you put together need to be able to trust each other's decisions, laud individual and team efforts, and learn to put their differences aside to work as a team. *How could you make that happen?*

You have to make each one of them realize the individual and collective importance they hold for the team. Like we said earlier, a team is like a well lubricated machine. You are the lubricant that ensures the smooth functioning of this machine and the members in your team are the components of that machine. Even if one of them falls out or malfunctions, the entire machine suffers. When employees acknowledge their importance in the team and know that they are trusted and appreciated by their team mates and lead, they tend to perform better – that inner motivation that we're so after comes out on its own!

Another important aspect of team building is to help the employees gauge the measure of their contribution to the team and the business. You could count it as an element of self- actualization where people are interested in knowing their share in the success of the organization. Being able to know that they single-handedly provided meaningful contribution to the organization they work for, that the success of their organization would not have possibly reached the level it is at currently had it not been for their contribution creates a positive impact on the level of employee engagement.

However, measuring employee contribution is unfortunately not that simple. It may be possible to gauge the share of individual; employees in the success of an educational institution or a hospital, but *what happens in the case of a retail organization?*

Let's take a look at how John Lewis the chain of high-end department stores in the UK manages this feat. According to John Lewis, they place great emphasis on their people – their employees are called partners –

and it is not just for the sake of it. Calling their employees "partners" helps establish a special bond between the employers and the employees.

Unlike employees who are limited to *"just do your work"*, partners share responsibilities for the customer care and greater outcomes of the business as a whole. So, John Lewis involves their "partners" in the decision making process and finding better solutions to the problems at hand. They empower their employees and in turn the employees take greater responsibility of their jobs and strive to make a difference – *the results? A revolutionized customer experience!*

Regular feedback is also prime to the establishment of healthy communication channels between the management and employees and building solid teams. However, most often the feedbacks commonly communicated are the negative ones.

Consider a scenario: you have been assigned an important project for the very first time. It's your first time working at something this big (read meaningful). Considering your inexperience, you manage to do a decent job at it after putting your heart and soul into the project. When you submit the project, the manager instead of lauding your effort points out a couple of small things you missed out on. This happens not once but twice – the manager does not appreciate the good things about your work, instead focuses on what it lacks. *Would you want to put in the same amount of commitment into the third project assigned to you?* There's a fat chance that you would not.

As a manager, your job is not only limited to setting targets, assigning tasks, and assessing performance. You have to be able to effectively coach the employees and shower them with praise wherever due and impart healthy criticism that can be taken constructively by the employee. Now let's see how the same scenario would inspire greater employee engagement if things were done slightly different than they were previously.

After you submit the project the first time, your manager mentions: *"This looks great! I knew you had it in you. We could make it even better if you add the following two considerations to the project..."*

When working on the second project you are mindful of not missing out on the points your manager highlighted in the first project. After submission your boss notices and lauds your effort of incorporating something he pointed out the last time. So when you work on the third project, you're by default much more confident, experienced, and motivated to take up the challenge! You know it's a learning, you know your effort will be recognized and appreciated, you know you have it under control – naturally your engagement in the project would be greater than it ever was.

Do you see the difference?

TRANSPARENCY

Like we mentioned before, communication is prime in bringing the people within an   organization close and helping them understand each other better. One of the objectives of effective communication is to promote better employee engagement. Managers are the visionaries of the organization. They are the ones who foresee the future of the company *(given everything works according to plan)* – and it is this vision that helps them set short- term goals for the organization and its employees.

Now the catch here is – *how can you expect active engagement from employees if they do not know what they are working for?*

Their job remains only a routine till the time they find a greater purpose for it. It is the realization of belonging to something greater than just a 9 to 5 routine. Managers need to properly communicate the clear vision they have for the organization. They need to tell their employees where the organization currently stands, where they wish to take it in the next five years, and how each employee through the accomplishment of their short-term goals can propel the organization to achieving its long term goals – turning the managers' visions into reality!

Employees need to understand the organization's goals, what they stand for, and why they are so important. They need to get a clearer picture of the business on the whole.

To ensure maximum engagement on the part of employees, it is therefore important that managers maintain clarity when it comes to highlighting the company's objectives and how each employee fits into the process of achieving these objectives. Clarity begins when leaders start conveying their thoughts and opinions to their employees in an appropriate manner.

So what's the difference between leaders and good leaders?

While leaders restrict themselves to clarifying their expectations to their employees and offer regular feedback on their performances, the good leaders go an extra mile to ensure that the employees have a proper process that can help them gain expertise on important tasks and facilitate their goal achievement process.

A fantastic example of this can be found in John Wooden the iconic UCLA basketball coach. He made it a habit to maintain detailed diaries on each player he coached during his remarkable career. These diaries kept a record of even the slightest improvements that in his opinion the players could make and did make. With that, he made it a point to share his views and thoughts with his players after each practice. The important thing to learn here is that good leaders work day-in day-out to hone the skills of their team. This leads to a series of small wins that culminate into an overall optimal performance delivered by the team as a whole.

You need to work on your people. Help them get better in what they're good at and achieve excellence in what they know best. It is the leader who pushes and inspires the employees to take a step further, to be a little more involved, and slightly more engaged in their work with every passing day.

Google by far has been the most successful organization to bring complete transparency in their work environment. Their culture focuses on bringing down the barriers that hinder the flow of creativity in the organization. They encourage their employees to be creative and collaborate their ideas for the collective sense of achievement.

The organization allows its employees the freedom to know their worth, improve what they're good at, and be in their element of creativity all the time. The organization believes transparency is only a small part of the culture they want in the organization. That combined with other elements of channeling behavioral habits of their employees towards their work and jobs has made sure Google's employees remain actively engaged in their jobs. They know what's expected from them, they know what the business is out to achieve, and they are putting in their all to help the organization move steadily towards its goals.

Would you believe if we told you that Google formally allows its employees to spend around 20% of their time at work doing things that do not fall in their regular work function? Because that is exactly what they do!

When we talk about transparency, there are two other things that demand attention. The thing is that transparency does not occur overnight. Where it is important for the leaders to establish a free-flowing route for communication between them and the employees, it is equally imperative for them to build the credibility of the organization in the eyes of the employees to increase their confidence in the place they work at.

Engagement is not something you can instill in the employees. It comes from within. It's like a plant that needs to be looked after, regularly watered, and provided with ample sunshine to grow and blossom. So where engagement is concerned, part of the nourishment it requires comes from a sense of belonging and pride. Your employees need to be proud of their jobs and the organization they belong to. For that, you need to set up a thriving reputation of the company backed by appropriate ethical standards that the company doesn't compromise on. You need to make the employees believe in the organization's purpose – something that adds value to what they do.

Take the example of Southwest Airlines. The organization went beyond its way to establish a meaningful purpose for their employees. They refused to be looked at as a simple airline company, they wanted depth to their business operations and so they promoted their reputation as an organization that helps people *"connect with what's most important to them"*.

Shunning their image as mere transporters, they worked on building an image that portrayed them as the "people" who enabled other people reach out to the people and places they value. This powerful purpose at some point connected with their employees who began seeing greater depth in their regular everyday jobs. It helped them connect to their purpose in the organization on an emotional level and eventually led to better engagement.

When it comes to developing a sense of confidence in the employees over their future in the company, managers have monumental task in front of them. You can't expect the employees to follow code, show up for work on time, or be dedicated to their job and the organization unless you yourself are doing all that. It makes a huge difference; employees, even the millennials would look up to you for guidance and course of action. You need to lead by example. Create an environment whereby, the employees know that if they want the future they desire, they need to act and work a certain way to achieve it.

Remember, if you're being negative about things around you, your employees will only follow course – you can't expect them to be actively engaged in their work process.

VISION

Each employee has a vision for their career – one they wish to achieve before retirement. Organizations promoting active people engagement in their culture tend to share their employees' vision and create an environment and opportunities that help them accomplish it.

There would be hardly an employee who does not want to progress in their career overtime. Career advancement is one of the many charms that can keep the employees motivated and highly engaged in their jobs – a definite tool to inspire active engagement of millennials. People look for meaningful jobs, ones that are challenging and provide them an adequate opportunity to show their potential and push their limits in addition to helping them learn more about their line of work.

It is getting a chance to explore their skills and trying new things that keep the jobs interesting for employee. Employees often look for organizations that offer proper job rotations and talent mobility to their best talent; they tend to prefer organizations that set stretch goals for their employees and hold them accountable for their progress. Another factor that influences employee engagement when it comes to career satisfaction is the presence of responsibility-enriched jobs. It matters to employees that they are trusted enough by their leaders to be assigned responsibilities that can have a greater impact on the organization as a whole. Just like we discussed earlier, the millennials want responsibility and the autonomy to see them through and make an actual difference. The same helps them stay actively engaged in their jobs and deliver their absolute best at all times.

When employees are allowed a certain level of control over their jobs, it acts like an instant boost to their level of engagement. However, allowing employees to exercise control demands greater flexibility on part of the managers. You have an employee who recently gave birth and is back at work realizing the importance of her role in the ongoing projects of the organization – *how do you pay her back for her loyalty?*

Obviously a recognition and positive feedback can lift her spirits but if you allow her the flexibility to take time off work to tend her child during work hours, it would go a long distance in ensuring that this employee stays actively engaged in her job. When we talk about giving employees control over their job, it is not just the working hours that need to be considered.

It is always a good idea to allow employees to have a say in their career progress and the company decisions that may directly impact them. They can be allowed autonomy to a certain level that gives them the liberty to take decisions and decide the course of things that they are in charge of. They should be allowed to express their opinion and the management needs to value it. The renowned Hyatt group of hotels has boasted stellar employee retention rates over the years. They have employees serving long tenures and being as actively engaged in their jobs as they always have been. *How do you think they manage that?*

Hyatt places increased focus on the development of their employees or "associates" as they prefer to call them. The management makes it a point to listen to and attempt to solve the problems of their employees in the process. They look for collective solutions and try to implement policies that address problems on a long term. This is how they win the loyalty and active engagement of their associates. This triggers the motivation that employees require from within that helps them stay committed to their jobs and organizations for a longer time.

Following their example, there are a number of organizations that are working towards employee development and incorporating useful measures to improve the overall level of engagement of their employees. With that let's move on to the last but most important principle of Active People Engagement – Accessible leadership.

ACCESSIBLE LEADERSHIP

We just discussed multiple concepts of leadership that directly or indirectly contribute to the improvement of employee engagement levels. All of the above mentioned concepts at the end of the day culminate into a much vaster phenomenon of the "open door policy".

Organizations are complex setups that work on the basis of the individuals they employ. These individuals often come from diverse backgrounds; have different sets of educational qualifications, and dissimilar temperaments and mentalities. To have all these people come together and work for a common objective can be a mammoth challenge for the organization's leadership.

If there is one thing that can bring all this together in harmony and have the organization functioning in complete harmony – it is the organization's culture. A culture is made up of the policies, beliefs, ideologies, and values of a given group of people – in this case it is the organization. Workplace culture defines the way the people of an organization collaborate and behave with other people in the organization.

For an organization, employees are the most valuable assets. The employees are the ones who turn the wheel of contribution that adds up to the overall productivity of the organization ensuring the accomplishment of its targets within the defined time frames. If it weren't for the employees, we wouldn't have witnessed corporate giants like Google and Microsoft achieving the heights of success like they have. Hence, it is unwise on the part of the management to ignore the concerns of their employees.

If the employees within your organization think of their job as nothing more than a source of earning regular income, there is no one to blame but you. You failed at creating a work environment and culture that makes your employees want to make their job a priority over other things in their lives. For employees to place confidence in their workplace and value their job it is necessary for them to work in cordial conditions.

This calls for transparency at all levels of the organizational hierarchy and effective communication channels to exchange information and address issues at hand in a better way. You need to basically promote a culture where none of the employees feel neglected or complain about their queries and issues not being heard by their bosses/management.

This entire scenario leads us to the concept of the *"open door policy".* Let's move on to finding out more about it.

As the name suggests, the open door policy refers to the steps an organization takes to ensure the availability of the management and superiors to their subordinates at all times. *How do they ensure that?* By keeping the doors to their offices open – ALWAYS! that includes everyone; the CEO's office too.

This concept sees closed doors as a barrier to the smooth flow of information within the organization. Therefore, the core purpose of the open door policy is to make sure that absolutely anyone from the junior employee to the team lead or even managers can walk up to their seniors as and when they want to discuss the issues they face or are facing.

An open door policy rejects the conventional role of the senior management to sit in isolated cabins and order employees around delegating work to them. Rather, it places them as fundamental pillars that are supposed to provide strong foundation for the employees to progress and grow. These managers have to be the pioneers of establishing healthy interaction between employees and promote a generally positive environment at the workplace.

In order to bring the best out of each employee, the management needs to make conscious efforts to address the problems of their employees, help them hone their skills, and grow professionally. *But how exactly does the open door policy help the organization?*

There are several benefits that come attached with the implementation of the open door policy:

An open door policy promotes effective communication between the management and its employees. This is something we have been stressing upon throughout the book. For the optimal functioning of the organizational setup it is extremely important that the information flows freely up and down the hierarchy, is understood, and timely acted upon.

Leaving the office doors open allows employees to acknowledge the accessibility of the management and refrains them from sinking into the feeling of being left out in a time of crises at the workplace. An employee who knows they can walk up to their management whenever they want to discuss something that bothers them will always be more loyal to and engaged in their jobs than the ones who have to think a hundred times before approaching the management.

The policy eliminates any chances of confusion. Since the employees have the opportunity to directly interact with their superiors on any given matter, work related problems and glitches can be resolved there and then. Besides that, employees are motivated to put in that extra level of dedication required to meet the expectations of their management. It promotes general goodwill in the work culture as employees see their management as their biggest support system.

The open door policy leads to healthy discussions. It is a great way for employees to put their ideas and innovative solutions forward for the management to consider. These discussions can be the perfect platform for drafting key policies that can later shape and influence the work culture into becoming more employee-focused and highly engaged. In addition to that, the employees get to learn from the experience and expertise of their seniors as these discussions at times take the course of mentoring sessions.

The open door policy establishes mutual respect between the management and the employees. We have already discussed how a dictatorial management style fails in the modern day corporate scenarios. When managers want to be respected, they can't just demand it or take the 'Hitler approach' into having the employees submit to their commands. They need to earn this request.

When managers allow open communication between them and the employees, they are giving the employees a chance to express themselves and be heard. The managers listen to the issues faced by the employees, respect their opinions, work with them to find plausible solutions, and collectively work alongside them for the greater good of the organization. This earns them the loyalty and respect of their subordinates. It also makes the employees to provide meaningful contribution to the organization's goals.

Implementing the open door policy also ensures that the employees have the chance to get a better understanding of the organization, its purpose, its objectives, and its operations. Any doubts or misconceptions over a matter can be provided with detailed feedbacks and appropriate policies to clarify them and keep the employees in the loop of the effective communication channel of the organization.

We know for a fact that the millennials will love the open door policy. They are big on feedback and do not quite appreciate red tapes. There might be a mixed response from the Gen X, in all honesty as some of them may see it as just another conniving move from the management to make them open up about what they think about their job or the management. For the boomers, most of them will have to change their ways of management from being autocratic to one that encourages input from the employees. For the most part, the things we just discussed under the "open door policy" would be more or less overlapping with the other three principles of Active People Engagement. It's true, these principles do overlap with each other at some point or another, but that is because if you pull even a single one of them out of the equation, your pursuit for actively engaging your employees may remain incomplete. They have to go hand in hand if you wish to improve the engagement scores of your employees.

We have discussed how managements can improve the engagement levels of their employees by incorporating the four (4) principles of Active People Engagement. It is now time to move to the strategies that can bring about serious results in improving engagement.

THE WORKING STRATEGIES OF EMPLOYEE ENGAGEMENT

There have been various studies which reveal that employees that are actively engaged are almost 50% more productive than the ones who aren't engaged or are disengaged. If nothing else, this should be real motivation for you to come up with potent strategies that engage the hearts, minds, and hands to improve their productivity.

There are different levels at which organizations can address this issue and overcome it. The strategies are designed to work independently and may have to be altered to work in collaboration with each other or to be aligned with overall business strategy of the organization. Keeping the above mentioned principles of active engagement in mind, you can implement one or a combination of the following strategies to improve the level of engagement in your employees.

PARTNER FOR PERFORMANCE SUPPORT

Performance support is best achieved through servant leadership. You essentially learnt the importance of establishing and maintaining a strong, healthy relationship between the management and the employees. *Now how exactly can you put this 'powerful bond' to its intended role?* You need to channel this positivity into a strategic program that helps you keep the employees motivated in the long run and trigger a process of result-oriented organizational performance.

For that, you need to provide robust performance support to the employees. You're already familiar with the different behaviors and motivational elements of your employees; now put that knowledge to use and help your employees understand how they and their behaviors concur with their performance goals.

The strategy takes a cascading effect. It is the senior leadership that identifies and sets the core objectives of the business. The managers in turn, set focused targets for their teams.

Once the team targets are set, the managers then collaborate with each individual team member to decide on their individual goals that will assess their performance. For this strategy to work, it is important that the performance management process is designed in a way that it facilitates the individual targets of the employees – these goals have to be SMART goals.

You want to make your employees actively engaged in their jobs? Create SMART goals for them individually and collective SMART objectives for the team as a whole to motivate and inspire them to give their best.

THE **SMART** METHODOLOGY

SMART is a widely used mnemonic acronym that sets the criteria of directing the goal setting function of the management.

Each letter in the mnemonic acronym stands for a property that makes objectives more focused and defined.

Here's what SMART means:

Specific: Goals need to be specific and clear, with no room for vagueness.

Measurable: These goals should be measurable in terms of progress, performance, time, quality, and quantity.

Attainable: They should be realistic and achievable given the level of control, caliber, and time frame for each employee.

Relevant: These goals need to add value to the overall business objective and the individual career of the employee.

Time bound: The goals need to have a defined time-limit for accomplishment. This is important for instilling better time management in the employees.

SMART HIRING

Did it ever cross your mind that if you put in a little extra effort at the time of hiring managers to ensure that the candidates you select are the ones share the core values and possess the leadership skills required by your company can actually make your life easier later?

This is a common practice among leading organizations that boast high levels of employee engagement. They begin their engagement improvement policies from the very start – the recruitment of managers. These organizations make it a point to hire people who have the leadership skills and values that align with the core values of the organization. This helps them pick employees that can ease into the company's culture and get along better with other like-minded employees.

For these organizations this is more important than hiring on the basis of job competency of the candidates. One may argue that this may not be bringing in the best talent in the organization; but look at it this way, even if you manage to secure the best talent for a vacancy in the organization, if they are unable to settle properly in the given culture of the organization, they wouldn't stick around for long – now that is a BIGGER problem!

Besides, there are greater chances of a team performing exceptionally well under managers who have natural leadership abilities, strong work ethic, and the genuine inclination of working along with the team to find the best possible solutions. Managers who are actively engaged tend to guide and shape the course to high-engagement levels in the organization by building and enhancing their relationship with the employees and the senior leadership.

The whole idea is for the managers to be able to identify the core values of the business and then align individual and team objectives with those values to inspire maximum engagement and optimal productivity from the employees.

You know what changes you need to make to your recruitment policies in order to hire the right breed of managers for your organization.

HUMAN DRIVEN COLLABORATIVE LEARNING PROGRAMS

We learnt earlier that employee engagement levels are, to a degree, directly proportional to the level of learning (training and development) they receive in their respective roles. It is what helps them gauge their individual growth over a given period of time. With everything entering the digital era in the business sphere, most organizations use the latest computer supported collaborative learning (CSCL) programs to develop and train their employees for future growth.

While there is no harm as such in using CSCL as a means of achieving employee development targets, it should be kept in mind that these programs lack the much required element of human interaction. When you're out to achieve optimum levels of engagement from your employees, you should be aware of the fact that employees automatically perform better when they are nurtured using techniques that they can connect with.

A CSCL program may be designed to be highly interactive and engaging for the employees – but let's face it, these employees spend all their day staring at the computer screen, and no matter how well designed your program is, it will not have the impact that human interaction can have. We're not saying that you need to go ahead and completely eliminate the CSCL program. You only need to take appropriate measures to introduce human driven collaborative learning (HDCL) in support of your CSCL program.

The concept of HDCL works in tandem with connecting real-life coaches with your employees. Someone who is well known: a high-profile industry figure who can connect at a better level with your employees than a simple computer program that gives out instructions and directions for better performance. Some examples of the use of this strategy goes back to the basics of the learning processes and engagement techniques used by schools when they have career days or by remarkable young professional organizations such as the Omaha Jaycees/Omaha Junior Chamber of Commerce and many others across the worlds when they have guest speakers at their events. It is simple; human interaction comes with the added benefit of real life examples and experiences – something that employees can visualize, have witnessed happening, or apply on themselves to see how they work – the CSCL lacks that.

Introduce regular coaching sessions in the organization, where you invite a notable person from the business community to inspire and guide your employees into improving their work ethics, their skills, and learning from the experiences from someone they can look up to and follow. These sessions do not have to be too long. Even a 30-minutes session focused on something worthwhile can make the difference; the rest can be taken care of with the CSCL program.

Once you have this established, work in your CSCL program as a support tool to reinforce the concepts, ideologies, and core ideas introduced and coached by the real-life mentors in their sessions. The mentors can deliver the basics of a concept and the CSCL can be designed to drill those concepts into your employees' minds and work styles. This will go a long way into ensuring that your employees have a sense of continuous learning and growth and will eventually have a positive impact on their level of engagement.

It is extremely important to make sure that both your HDCL and CSCL programs are synchronized with each other to bring the desired impact on employee behavior.

THE POWER OF TEAMWORK

We already established in the previous chapter that teamwork is an important element of Active People Engagement. However, if the organization at any point in time fails to harness the real power of teamwork, it's as good as non-existent for the business. The real essence of teamwork is the proper utilization of each individual talent in the team for the collective achievements of goals (both individual and organizational).

A team-based organizational structure has all the basic ingredients required to make the most of active employee engagement. Here's how:

For teams to be successful, the members need to communicate effectively, interact and collaborate with other members of the team in order to achieve their objectives. So, *how exactly do you harness the actual potential of teamwork that leads to higher engagement levels?*

You build and promote an environment of trust. A study conducted by Sandra L. Robinson *(professor at University of British Columbia in Vancouver, Canada)* and Sabrina Deutsch Salamon (*associate professor at York University in Toronto, Canada)* back in 2011 revealed that employees who felt trusted by their management and colleagues showed better prospects of meeting their team lead/manager's expectations and excel in overall performance. The study was conducted on 88 Canadian retail stores where performance is judged on the basis of customer service and sales.[29]

When one establishes a culture of mutual trust in the teams and the organization, it triggers the element of ownership and respect. Employees recognize the worth

[29] www.blog.shrm.org/workforce/trusting-employees-supports-better-performance-research-finds

of belonging to a team; consider other members of the team as *"my people"*; there is a considerable decrease in the *"my job, his job"* as employees feel responsible towards their own as well as the collective actions of the team. There is no chance of blame games and what you have is a team of talented individuals, who are ready to put their differences aside, trust each other's abilities, take responsibility for the task at hand, and respect the differences in each other's opinion to achieve the greater good – in this case the targets of the team that can only be accomplished when they complete their individual goals.

It is important to note here that instilling trust and increasing collaborative efforts in the team alone will not bear the fruit you wish to harvest. For building a high-performance team where every individual team member is actively engaged, you as the manager need to empower the employees. You need to let go part of your leadership and effectively distribute it among your employees based on their individual and the team's collective performance against the present goals set for them. For this, you obviously need to leverage the forte of each member in your team for optimal results.

To achieve employee engagement with teamwork, carefully divide the workforce into potent teams under the leadership of an able manager who has the foresight and the capability to steer the ship in the right direction.

ATTAINING EMPLOYEE INVOLVEMENT

Most would assume that employee involvement and employee engagement are more or less the same thing. Well, they're not. There's a distinct line between the two that separates them. While employee engagement is the term that is used to highlight the connection between an organization's employees and its visions and objectives; involvement refers to the active pursuit of the said objectives on the part of employees.

Employee involvement is that element of the game plan that can make or break the entire outcome of the organization's initiative to promote active engagement among its employees. It is what transfers the ownership of ideas and initiatives from the hands of the senior management to the offices of the executives.

Simply put, attaining employee involvement entails allowing the executives to be a part of the decision making process. It's about granting them the liberty to express and own their ideas and take decisions for the best possible execution of these ideas. Employee involvement means that you are providing your employees a chance to merge their vision with that of the company, you're allowing them the ownership of their thoughts and ideas, instilling a feeling of belonging that will go a long way in ensuring that the same employees remain loyal to the organization, share its vision, and do whatever it takes to transform that vision into reality.

Now employee involvement is not something that can be attained overnight. The key here is to make sure the employees do not feel like they are only executing a vision that belongs to someone else.

When you give the employees a chance to be heard, be involved in the decision making processes of the company, and own up their ideas and responsibilities, it automatically adds up to their engagement level.

Employee involvement at times may involve strategies that suggest you give up part of your control in the hands of the employees. While this may be a tough call to make, if you are confident about the talent you have working for you and the policies that are in place to manage it, there isn't much you need to worry about.

THE VALUE OF SHARING AND GIVING

Most of the strategies for improving levels of employee engagement are based on promoting general positivity in the organizational culture. They are focused on creating an environment that helps the employees connect with each other, maintain an optimistic outlook on the things around them, explore and improve their existing skills, and give all they've got to the task at hand for as long as they are at work.

An extremely important function of establishing an environment as such is the concept of *"sharing"*. It's obvious that the resources available in an organization have to be shared by the employees, but there is a resource greater than all that – knowledge!

Professional knowledge comes from experience and sharing that knowledge can encourage learning and a sense of accomplishment in the employees. It can help them grow professionally and improve their chances of overall growth. It will also give them a boost in self-actualization that promotes a feeling of accomplishment.

A number of organizations create knowledge pools where employees can share research, studies, field relevant data, and other informative resources that they work on or come across with other employees in their team or with the organization as a whole. This way, it's not just one person who's learning – it's the entire organization – collective growth!

Similarly, when it comes to giving it is all about enhancing the self-actualization of the employees. Giving back is a universal way of feeling accomplished in bringing about a positive change in the society. Many organizations run employee driven community welfare programs that are meant to bring a difference to the environment and/or the community.

These may include a number of activities like volunteering at old age homes, running a marathon as a support for disease awareness, bi-annual blood donation drives, or go-green initiatives that employees can participate in as an added function of their job responsibility. To make these programs more comprehensive, organizations often allow the different teams organize and execute the initiative – this obviously includes everything from deciding when, how, where, and why to the more important who is in charge of what.

Whether co-created or individual, workplace giving programs can provide an instant boost to the overall engagement levels of the employees and are definitely worth the resources and efforts an organization puts in them.

EMPLOYEE WELL-BEING

There are no doubts over the fact that the happier and healthier your employees are the more engaged and more productive they tend to be. Health is of primary importance. You need your workforce to be healthy and active; and while it may be a personal initiative to stay healthy in most cases, a little contribution by the organization for maintaining employee health can work wonders for the organization.

Employee well-being assures that the organization has high productivity levels and minimum absences. A number of organizations take initiatives to facilitate the well-being of their employees. While some may do that by conducting regular health check-ups, others might take to installing an on-premises gym or providing healthy meals at discounted rates. Also, organizations employ integrated employee assistance and innovative work-life balance programs to help employees grow and sustain better.

A number of wellness support initiatives that include stress management experts, parenting groups, relationship counseling, money management programs, and more have helped different organizations connect with their employees at a different level, something that is far more valuable than the professional link between the two.

So how does this work for the employees?

Consider yourself as a hardworking employee who spends most of their time at work. You have a family that you can hardly manage to give time to, your health is declining and you don't have the time to visit a doctor; you want to join the gym or go for a run after work but you're way too exhausted when you get home after work. Your spouse does not appreciate your lack of interest in the family and that has pushed your marriage on the rocks – *would you be a happy person?*

Obviously not! So you approach your manager and try to make him understand the situation you are in. Now there are two types of managers: one that listens and understands your problem and assures you saying *"I'll see what we can do about this, for now I can allow you flexible work timings so that you can resolve your matters at home;"* the other type does listen to your problems but replies *"that's your personal issue, there isn't much we can do about it."*

It is obviously the first type of managers that will help you overcome your problems. They are concerned about your well-being, they want you to be productive at work and acknowledge the fact that you cannot be optimally productive unless your issues are solved first.

Of course you're not the only employee going through these problems; there will be more like you. And the proactive managers will try to come up with policies that facilitate their employees' health and well-being to ensure their maximum productivity and commitment to the organization. The other type of manager will simply expect you to manage the matters on your own and get back to work.

So which type of manager would you be more loyal to? Or rather let's put it this way: *which type of manager would you be willing to work for?* Obviously the one who is more concerned about you!

This is how focusing on employee well-being can win you their loyalty and ultimately higher levels of engagement.

RECOGNITION AND REWARD

We humans crave recognition. It is an inborn need that we have. We want to be appreciated for the good we do and being rewarded for it is the ultimate motivation for continuing to do good. Employees at a workplace are no different. Recognition and reward form part of almost all the text written by far on the science behind successful organizations.

Employee recognition encourages a healthy relationship between the managers and the employees and has proven to be an effective tool in improving the engagement level of the employees. However, it is important that the process of recognizing and rewarding the employees is done right to assure maximum effectiveness.

Experts suggest that there are three basic elements for effective employee recognition:

- Right behavior

- Right time

- Right way

Let's have a look at each of them in detail.

THE RIGHT BEHAVIOR

This is nothing out of the usual. The right behavior refers to any and all actions that lead to the accomplishment of performance objectives set for the individual keeping in mind the individual's career aspirations and their alignment to the company's objectives. There could be a number of things that qualify as the right behavior. These may include:

- Achieving or exceeding the pre-set targets in terms of quantity and quality of work

- Acquiring the skills and expertise of a new work procedure or process

- Demonstrating coherence with the core cultural values of the organization especially in context to the relationship with other employees

- Taking up a course of action that actually adds value to the organization

THE RIGHT TIME

It is important for the recognition to come at the right time. An early recognition will probably distract the employee from the task at hand and providing recognition too late may not be valued as much as it should be and would fail to have the desired impact on the employee – that is an improvement in their level of engagement.

So what is the right time for recognition?

It is commonly accepted that the best time for effective employee recognition is the time when they are working on or actually achieving the performance goal in question. This makes the employee realize that they and their efforts are being duly observed and appreciated and gives them the incentive to be more committed to accomplishing their performance objectives. *So make sure you time the recognition right for optimum results.*

THE RIGHT WAY

It is important to make sure the recognition is coming in the right ways. Saving it all up to be delivered at an annual event will not do justice to the purpose of effective employee recognition. It should be imparted on a regular basis. Statistics show that around 43% of the highly engaged employees are those who receive feedback from their management at least once in a week. On the contrary, only 18% of the employees with low engagement level receive regular feedback from their managements.[30]

Making sure you provide timely recognition and feedback to your employees can play a significant role in taking their level of engagement a notch higher. It can be the very difference between an engaged and disengaged workforce.

With that, let's wrap up this part of the section. You now have the knowledge and an outline of strategies that can help you improve the engagement level of your employees. If you take a closer look at everything that we've discussed so far, you'd notice that most of them would sit well with the *'problem generation' – the millennials.* Although these strategies are long standing and not specifically designed for the millennials, they will still work in engaging them better.

Why?

Let's recap the obvious traits of Generation Y. These young people are big on socializing and believe in open communication *(teamwork and smart hiring).* The millennials want to be recognized for their efforts and

[30] https://www.officevibe.com/blog/disengaged-employees-infographic

adequately rewarded for them too *(recognition and reward)*. The millennials are keen on growth by learning and acquiring better knowledge and skills in addition to being inclined towards giving back to the community to bring positive change in the society *(facilitated sharing and giving programs)*. Above all, they look for flexibility and that can be provided through strategies and programs aimed at employee wellbeing.

At the end of the day, what you have is a highly motivated workforce that is actively engaged in their jobs and providing the organization with the best they've got. It is up to you how you implement these strategies and see them work through. When making policies that define these strategies, make sure you do not have anything contradicting or overlapping the other – this may lead to inefficient policies that are unable to fulfill their purpose.

With employee engagement properly dealt with, it is now time for us to move to the concept of intrapreneurship and the different techniques that can help you create an innovative culture in the organization.

In organizations where curriculum, discipline, and uniformity form part of their core values, creativity becomes a victim. Most modern organizations do not realize that in an attempt to bring order to the workplace the creativity of their employees dies a slow, painful death.

The previous generations may have made peace with that but the millennials are not ready to settle.

This leads to the greater challenge of retaining the best talent within the organization. Besides that, creativity and innovation has become an absolute necessity for organizations to survive the cutting-edge competition in the markets/industries they operate in. What they need is a robust plan to encourage employees to be creative and bring in new, unique ideas for the improvement of the business and its operations. Hence the concept of facilitated intrapreneurship was introduced.

Here's a quick recap: *intrapreneurship occurs when employees within an organization adopt an entrepreneurial way of thinking when performing their assigned roles in the company.*

The deal is simple; if you do not provide adequate initiatives and opportunities for your employees to use their complete talent and potential, there will come a point where they will quit their job for something better – in most cases, a startup of their own. *You don't necessarily want that!*

The question that needs to be addressed at this point is: what can you do about it?

The first thing you need to realize is that instilling intrapreneurship in your employees requires a culture that promotes talent and competitive advantages. There are several things that can be done to achieve that. Let's take a look at what these things include:

ELIMINATING FEAR

Fear can drive out any possible ideas and innovations that an employee may have up their sleeves. Failure in most organizations is looked down upon as a waste of resources – to an extent it even is. However, failure brings the important element of learning with it. When the employees fear rebuke over their failure, it prevents them from trying out new things. You've got to make sure that does not happen.

Create an environment where the employees can attempt tasks and jobs in a way they see fit. Most conventionalists would argue *"what if it doesn't work?"* The possibility of it not working is a legit one, but then there's also a chance that their way of approaching the same job works – and works better than the way it was being done for years!

You need to give the employees a chance. The chance to put their brains and creativity to use and come up with something that can change the way you do things around the workplace simply because they are less complex, less time consuming, and as effective as your previous way of working.

There is obviously a catch that certain employees do not succeed in any of their attempts and cause huge losses in terms of productivity and resources – allowing them continuous failure isn't wise either. What you need to do is come up with a policy that allows the employees to put their creative minds to work and try new things but limit the number of failures until the employee can work through the causes of failure if at all possible.

For example: employee A is delegated a task which he thinks would take too much time if done conventionally. He takes the initiative that according to him would save time on the task but fails. Allow him a second chance to try something different, if he fails the second time you can simply direct him back to the conventional way. But here's the catch – after he fails the first time, he will try to make the most of his second chance. He will make it a point to go through the things he did wrong in his previous attempt, work on them, and do what it takes to make his strategy work this time around. And there's a greater possibility that he will succeed this time.

From where we see it, you have a win-win situation at hand. You're allowing the employees to let go off their fear of failure and develop their professional abilities employing innovation and creativity, and you're getting your hands on a pool of different ideas that can actually bring you the competitive advantage you need to surpass your competitors.

TEAM BUILDING

Yet again, we are revisiting the concept of 'teams'- it should be adequate for you to size up the importance of it! Team building is a great way to promote healthy competition and innovation within the organization. This works especially well with organizations that deal in multiple products and/or services.

When building teams to encourage a competitive work environment, you need to realize that comparison and competition is best between two people/groups of the same or equivalent caliber. Organize teams by appropriately grouping your workforce into self-sufficient balanced groups that have the capability of collectively handling the tasks that will be delegated to them.

Have one team focus on one thing – a product, a service, or a market niche. Allow them to put their ideas to work and come up with plans, strategies, and tools that they feel will help them oust the other teams in the organization. The best team obviously gets the best appraisals. So you have the competition, you have the playground, you have the rewards, there are no defined rules except for "fair play" – and you get to be the referee.

It is now up to the teams to come up with a creative game plan that can help them succeed. Team leads get to play a pivotal role at this point. In addition to providing their teams with proper guidance and direction, they also have the responsibility of assessing the performance of each member in the team. This is important because it is easier to recognize and laud the team effort of a group of individuals and it does contribute to their individual assessments as well, but when it comes to evaluating the individual performance of an employee in the group, things get difficult. This calls for regular feedbacks and updates on the part of the team lead, and eventually the senior management of the organization.

A good way about it is to hold regular assessments through quarterly meetings for all the teams. This way, you can stay updated on the latest developments and initiatives that the teams are working on, the effectiveness of any previous strategies that they have implemented, and the overall success of the team on collaborating on the job assigned to them.

So what do the organizations get out of this?

First, you have the entire workforce working towards a common objective – the accomplishment of organizational goals. In addition to that, the teams are working to the best of their abilities employing their talents, expertise, skills, and ideas to come up with the most cost and time efficient ways of executing the task at hand. This if looked upon overall is saving the organizations resources by making the most of the human capital and talent pool available within the premises.

ENCOURAGE INNOVATIVE INPUT

You're hiring talented employees, but not giving them a chance to use their talent for the greater benefit of the organization – *how is that fair to the individual and to the organization in general?* Your employees can be your most lucrative assets if you learn to capitalize on their talents and abilities and in order to learn that, you need to inculcate the habit of questioning and being open to discussion in the management and the overall work environment.

See, quarterly meetings and assessments are not just restricted to judging the performance of the employee. It is a great time to get to know what the employee feels about the business, its operations, its progress, and its future. Believe it or not, the same employees that work day in day out to steer the organization towards its goals on a steady pace, have the capability of coming up with ideas that can actually speed up the process in the most legit ways. These ideas and innovation at times are ones that do not cross the mind of the organization's policy makers and decision takers.

When you create an environment that is open for discussion, you are basically giving your employees an opportunity to come forward with their suggestions and ideas that can provide you with an additional perspective of looking at a particular matter.

Let's suppose you have to take a decision over the possibility of a new product launch. You currently have two different products that you are considering. The financials for both products show the same feasibility for the organization and give a healthy forecasted ROI. Experts in the organization are more inclined towards product (A) that targets a different market than product (B) – they see a better scope there. However, the sales team is pushing for the launch of product (B).

At this point if you ignore the point of view of your sales executives there may be a possibility that out are missing out a significant element related to the market, the competition, the target group, or the product type that may make have a drastic effect on your decision making process.

A simple question *"Which product do you think the company should launch?"* can lead to an insightful discussion and a plethora of ideas that can compel you enough to change your initial decision. Allowing employee input can go a long way in determining how you compete in the market and how well do you utilize the talent pool available to you.

CREATE OPPORTUNITY AND ROLL OUT THE INCENTIVES

As a leader/manager/entrepreneur, you have the inherent responsibility of creating sufficient opportunities for the employees to showcase their talent and intrapreneurial tendencies. Verbal encouragement may trigger the employees' motivation to actually present ideas and innovation their minds brew up, but unless they have a proper structure to put them forward and a chance to make them happen, there would always be something lacking.

If you have the resources to develop and manage a separate department – we say you set one up for the planning and processing of internal business ventures. This department can be used as a forum to invite and encourage employees to submit their innovative plans and ideas that can help the business improve its processes and productivity on the whole. This could simply begin with a plan to cut down unnecessary expenditure by employing a tech savvy tool/gadget that the organization wasn't aware of; and go all the way to complex plans and ideas for expansion and increase in operational capacity of the business.

Fact is people think differently. It is very rare to find two people who think in the exact same way. Every brain works in its own unique way; this is how ideas are born. What one person is capable of thinking at one point may occur to another later in time – but then it's the timing that actually matters. Ideas and innovation are only as good as their relevancy at the time they are presented in. Setting up an internal business venture planning department would allow employees to submit their creative suggestions and ideas as and when they occur to them. This will allow the department to put into action the ideas that are crucial to the given business scenario and can bring about a positive change in the organization.

That settled, you now have the department set up but how do you encourage the employees to put their thinking caps on and focus on matters other than the tasks assigned to them to come up with something that helps improve the overall working conditions in the organization? They need motivation and incentive.

When it comes to deciding on incentives and motivational tools, you need to be smart

about your choices. We've discussed earlier that each generation is attracted to and motivated by different things. The millennials may want instant recognition and a chance to put their idea into an action plan and then see its correct execution all by themselves; but the Gen X would rather have a company-paid short camping trip to the nearest National Park with their family.

It is up to you to decide what incentives and rewards you wish to shower your talented employees with. As long as you're making sure it is something of actual value to the employee in question – you'll be fine. Using the same policy for everyone would only lead to a waste of resources if it is not generating the desired results – in this case pushing employees to get creative with their work and bring new relevant ideas to the business.

A CREATIVE ENVIRONMENT

This strategy may not sit well with you if you are a strong supporter of work discipline and office curriculum. But if you are out to capture creativity at its best, you need to lure it with the environment that helps it flourish. What we'll need is a whole lot of fun backed by open praises and some powerful shots of positivity.

Encourage humor, play, and fun in the work environment. Set up relaxing zones where people can take a break and indulge in activities other than their job-related tasks. You need an environment that makes employees wake up every day eager to get to work. Let them breathe and enjoy the work they do.

When you provide employees with a free environment it allows them the space and time to think creatively. You can never extract creativity out of a stressed mind. Excessive rules, policies, and procedures tend to suffocate the talent your employees possess. They are so drained out by the way things are and the way they're supposed to be that they hardly have the time to think of something that can make the same procedures less stressful and time consuming – don't do that to your employees.

There could be several things you could do to set up a creative environment at the workplace. First off, start praising all the positive individual and group developments. If you have an in-house newsletter published on a monthly basis, make it a point to mention and highlight the innovative developments that took place over the month and make it a point to give due credits to the person/team that forwarded the idea.

Have creative sessions during afterhours or whenever convenient where you encourage employees to interact with each other. Encourage them to express, brainstorm, and discuss their views about the company's current performance and the ways in which they could bring improvement to them. When a group of people indulge in a discussion or a brainstorming session, there is a burst of ideas born that are backed by different perspectives and notions. One or some of them can actually prove worthwhile for the organization and the accomplishment of its goals.

Set up a gaming room where the employees can go play or simply sit back and relax their mind during work hours. This in addition to improving the level of their productivity increases the creative span of their minds. You could also establish a tradition for monthly or bi-annual office parties that allow employees to be themselves, share their thought and ideas with their colleagues outside the work-relationship, dress up and exchange gifts. If you're thinking all this is pointing too much towards employee well-being – *you're right!*

Ensuring employee well-being can actually encourage innovative thinking and intrapreneurship in the people of your organization. *You want your employees to take up an entrepreneur-like approach towards their respective work and departments?* Give them what they need to put that frame of mind into action.

PRIORITIZING CREATIVITY

Intrapreneurship is heavily dependent upon creativity. While it is extremely important for organizations to nurture and promote the existing talent in the organization to extract their best potential for the overall improvement of the organization and for obtaining the competitive edge that allows them to best their competition; the importance of constantly upgrading the level of creativity in the organization is tantamount.

One may be tempted to ask: *why?*

The answer is simple. Technology and innovation if left like they are go obsolete after a certain time period. It needs to be leveled up, it needs to be recharged. These two elements are crucial for the sustenance of valuable creativity   and   the   resulting   intrapreneurship organizations need to make the best use of the talent they have at hand.

So how do you upgrade the level of creativity in the organization? There could be two ways to do it:

1. Internal efforts

2. Bring in some competition

All the intrapreneurship strategies that we have been discussing above can be applied as internal efforts to achieve improvement in the existing talent. In addition to those, one can   conduct training sessions on a regular basis that help employees develop a creative way of thinking. Keeping a track of, informing and educating the workforce on the latest developments in research and technologies can go a long way to achieve the same purpose. In addition to all that, you can also make it a habit to send your staff to external creative exhibits and competitions that improves their creative compatibility. There's a lot that can be done to make and encourage employees take up the creative route to reach their and consequently the organization's goals.

These initiatives can effectively brew up internal competition among the employees *(a solid system for incentives and rewards will play a pivotal role in determining the level of competition)*. However, there will always come a point where the employees become accustomed to the competition they face within the organization. Truth is not all employees are as creative, as smart, or as talented as the others. There is also the consideration that an employee's talent is judged on the basis of their abilities.

Simply put, employee A and employee B could be equally creative and talented; but where Employee A is good with the strategic aspect of things, employee B may have a better hold on the technical aspects of the same thing. You can't really compare them both on the same given scale. That said, it is also possible that employee C is great at their job but does not indulge in taking up opportunities as they come or make use of them for furthering their given knowledge and skills.

Now when we talk about internal competition, it is not just the managers that are noticing these diversities. There will come a point where the employees will become aware of who their real competition is and who is not even near their league. When a time like this approaches, organizations will witness even the best of their talents becoming laid back

– a time where incentives wouldn't be able to extract more out of them either. *You don't* want this to happen! So what do you do?

You bring in more competition. The very next logical question to follow this revelation should be how organizations can actually accomplish that feat. You need to tap external sources to import talent and creativity into the business. There are a handful of strategies to make that happen.

The very first one begins at the time of new recruitments. When hiring new individuals, don't just focus on the right person for the right job at the right time – look for the creativity too. You can judge a person's creativity by analyzing their answers or responses to hypothetical situations that compel them to think out of the box, come up with something unique, and take a problem-solving approach to the issue at hand. When you make it a point to bring in creative individuals in the organization with every hiring process, existing employees know they're up against the money to be as creative as they possibly can to win the rewards you've set for them.

You could also tap into external sources of talent by introducing internship programs in collaboration with universities. The deal is simple: You get a fresh batch of talented young individuals working at your organization *(even if it is for a short time period)* and you send in a couple of your employees over to the universities to brief the students about practical work experiences.

What you get here is creative young people bringing in a burst of enthusiasm and whacky ideas that can actually prove worthwhile at times. The employees you send over at universities get a different kind of exposure than the ones they normally get and possibly different perspectives of looking at things when they engage in a dialogue with the students. Besides, there is always the added charm of new competition to keep your employees on their toes to capitalize on every opportunity thrown their way.

If you thought that is all, it's not! There is more. This strategy is ideal for organizations aiming to expand their operations to reach out to a wider customer base. Mergers and acquisitions count as two of the most popular expansion policies whereby an organization either joins hands or acquires another similar organization in order to grow stronger or improve its market share. But there is another extremely important thing that happens with mergers and acquisitions – new employees become part of the organization!

Most of these new employees have been part of the other organization for a while. They are aware of their way around the tasks at hand and bring a new set of techniques, tools, and cultural aspects to the organization. It makes the organizational mix more diverse and with diversity comes competition. It's actually not just the competition that heats up with the advent of new employees; the same become a source of various strategies and work- related solutions that weren't part of the existing work culture of the organization.

This helps set up a competitive work environment whereby all employees have to put in their absolute best to be acknowledged – it basically leaves them not much choice except for bringing their best ideas forward.

With that, we'd wrap up this chapter in strategies to encourage intrapreneurship and creativity within the organization. Our next chapter will look into the different aspects of bringing about improvement in talent mobility within the organization before we move forward to combining all these things up into one solid talent management module for modern day organizations and their millennial dilemma.

Effective talent management is all about development of employees for future leadership. Talent mobility is just one of the tools that can help organizations achieve their desired talent management objectives.

Here's a quick recap: the concept of talent management encompasses the rotation of employees through different functions of the organization giving them the opportunity to hone their existing skills and acquiring new ones that prepare them for general leadership.

We're not saying that talent mobility is the only way for leadership development; neither do we claim that it is the most effective tool for this feat. Rather, the model has its own detailed set of drawbacks that at times can derail organizational operations. Moving employees from one department/function to another can have two extreme outcomes: either it works or it fails – but it fails only when mobility is not done right.

We've previously established in detail how mobility of talent can prove to be a legitimate tool for managers and organizations for developing their existing employees for future leadership. But like we just mentioned, it is imperative that the mobility module followed by the organization is based on genuine facts that guide their decisions to move the employees around the enterprise. This chapter will talk about everything you need to know about setting up a talent mobility framework that actually works for your organization.

Before we move on to the nitty-gritty of the matter it is important to mention how impressively Marriott International deals with talent mobility throughout the organization. The secret lies in judging and evaluating employees for a strategic fit in different functions of the company operations. With around 3,000 lodging properties across the globe and operations in over 70 countries – Marriott International is a colossal organization that has ample scale and opportunities to experiment with internal talent mobility as a device for leadership development – and it has been doing great so far.

Managers at Marriott International are aware of the fact that their development would be the outcome of a series of assignments that vary in nature and complexity. Ideally, talent mobility can be practiced/experienced in two different ways: within-property movements *(generally happen when employees are transferred from one function to another)*; and inter-property *(when employees are transferred from one property of the business to another)*. Marriott practices both and in high volumes. These movements are capable of wreaking havoc within the organization but for Marriott they have been contributing a solid foundation for high performance and stability.

So how does talent mobility work wonders for Marriott?

It helps them retain employees within the organization – so there is essentially little or no talent drain. When Marriott rotates people in different functions and properties, it adds to the experience and knowledge of the employees. It's adding value to their career and indirectly contributing to their growth as a professional. As a result, the employees want to stick with the organization and grow with it. This gives Marriott International a ready-to-takeover pool of leaders. These employees are capable of stepping up and taking charge of positions that demand more responsibilities and commitment whenever the need arises.

In addition to employee retention, Marriott also witnessed an improvement in the overall performance of the organization that stemmed from the positive impacts of talent mobility throughout the different properties of this corporate giant. Normally, when managerial positions in a company become vacant the overall operations of the business face the consequent turbulence that although short-term is capable of wreaking havoc on the collective performance of the organization. Marriott faced no such drawbacks.

The developmental gains of mobility proved adequate to absorb the shocks of managerial vacancies in the organization. With in-house employees ready to perform in managerial positions, the organization saved itself from incurring huge business losses or a downturn in the productivity levels. When it comes to making mobility decisions, the discretion does not solely lie in the hands of the management. There are a number of external factors (primarily market forces) that influence the decisions. A good management will consider these external factors in depth before making the move.

For a mobility model to be successful, it is important that the decision makers base their decisions solely on facts. These facts could relate to the prevailing conditions of the market, the down performance of a particular function, the superior leadership skills of certain employees, the pool of unique talent that the organization has. However, this alone wouldn't have the desired impact unless the management knows how to use these facts and turn them into a favorable strategy for the business and the accomplishment of its goals.

This takes us to establishing the significance of the mobility equation. Before an organization goes on to design a mobility model for their employees it is imperative that they get a better understanding of the mobility equation and how it works.

UNDERSTANDING THE MOBILITY EQUATION

The mobility equation has three basic elements. These elements can be shaped into three simple questions, which when answered can lay down the foundations for a talent mobility program in the organization. Once the structure is complete, organizations can make alterations to it in order to create a model that is customized according to their requirements.

So if you wish to develop a talent mobility strategy for your organization, you need to get the answers for these simple questions:

- What type of mobility does the organization need?

- Who needs to be mobilized?

- How much mobility does the organization require?

Now let's take a look at each of these questions in detail.

WHAT TYPE OF MOBILITY DOES THE ORGANIZATION NEED?

Mobility can be achieved at different levels in different forms. For example, employee A can be transferred to another branch/franchise of the organization that is at a different location in the country or in a different country altogether without any change in his function or position. This will change the surroundings for them, provide them a different cultural exposure and add to their business knowledge at different levels.

On the other hand, employee B can be transferred from one function of the business to another within the same premises. Now this would help employee B focus on building their capabilities that can later add to their skill pool and give them well-rounded knowledge of different functions to may be take a leadership position for one in the future.

This variable of the equation demands close consideration of the end objectives that the management wishes to achieve with the planned mobility. These objectives at times may be a result of alterations in the business strategy or other market related issues that may give rise to the possibility of looking into talent mobility as a viable solution.

Take the example of a company who is looking to make a strategic paradigm shift towards eco-friendlier business processes. This, among other things requires the organization to develop internal talent employing between-business mobility of employees to achieve the end objective. When the human capital management assesses the available talent pipeline in the organization they realize that there is a lack of a capability in the organization that is essential for the accomplishment of eco-friendliness in the processes – this could be a technical expertise or the professional knowledge required to see the processes through. The organization can resort to geographical mobility to deal with the lack of technical expertise, while a change of function could bring the required knowledge of the processes to accomplish this feat.

Once the organization knows its intended purpose of mobility, the next question that needs an answer is related to the dilemma of which employees need to make the move.

WHO NEEDS TO BE MOBILIZED?

There could be two ways to decide on the answer to this question. Companies can either take a contest-mobility approach or a sponsored-mobility approach.

The contest-mobility approach creates an equal opportunity for employees who wish to compete for promotions to prove their mettle for possible internal transfers in the organization. This type of mobility can bring in that extra push of motivation that may encourage the employees to go an extra mile in an attempt to surpass the performance of others, but it comes with a drawback – it will also make the competitive nature of the policy compel employees into not co-operating with other employees in the process.

Contrary to the contest-mobility approach the sponsored-mobility approach centers the investment of the company in candidates that exhibit the highest leadership potential. This type of mobility works well for organizations that have a solid structured process for identifying potential candidates for leadership development, nurturing, and retaining them after a series of rotations through the organization. It is something Marriott International excels at!

Now we're not saying that both of these approaches to mobility are mutually exclusive. They can be combined to draw up a stellar strategy for talent mobility, but the effectiveness of this strategy will depend on the right use of the right strategy at the right time. This leads us to the second consideration that needs your attention while answering this question: the eligible employees.

You basically need to have a clear idea of the managerial level of employees who can be considered for the said mobility.

Do you need the early-career employees to help them familiarize themselves to the processes and environment of the business and simultaneously build on their skills and capabilities as they experience different functions within the organization; or a mid-career employee would be more suited to be developed professionally so that he can be set on the path to career growth?

HOW MUCH MOBILITY DOES THE ORGANIZATION REQUIRE?

After the important elements of what sort of mobility is required and who is required to be mobilized, the next challenge an organization faces is to decide on how much mobility would be favorable for it at a given point in time. This is crucial! Organizations need to create a balance between the amount of mobility they activate and the time frame it has to adhere to.

Pushing for too much mobility in too little time will only lead to disasters – this is the exact chaotic drawback of talent mobility we mentioned earlier. When employees are transferred from one place/position to another, they take time to settle in and get accustomed to the workings in their new surroundings. This is one reason why the benefits of a talent mobilization cannot be capitalized upon until a certain amount of time has passed.

Another thing that deserves consideration in this matter is the number of times a developing leader has made an internal move over the course of their employment. *Is the number sufficient for their desired career growth? Are they too many in a short time span to allow them to fully capitalize on the learning they acquire from each move?*

While the above mentioned questions would help you deduce the eligibility of a certain employee for the said mobility program; others like: what should be the percentage of talent that could be moved in a one-year period? Is one international move enough for an employee to gain the cultural breadth necessary for the future role as a manager? Or is it necessary to provide an all-segment exposure to a candidate for sales management? – can help you just where you need to pull the plug on the number of mobility programs in the on-going business operations.

According to experts, an employee undergoing leadership development training needs to spend at least two years in the same position/post to be able to truly acquire the knowledge they need and learn from their experiences before moving on to their next assignment. This requires the management to have a strong hold on their talent pool and a greater insight of the areas of the business that need developmental gains of mobilization.

It is important to remember that regardless of the strategies you draw, there will always be trade-offs – the solutions to the organization's problems will be contextual, mainly depending on how efficiently you plan the mobility program for your desired objectives.

Organizations need to bring their A-game forward when it comes to talent assessment and situation analysis that can determine a robust strategy for talent mobility and later payback in the terms of improved employee retention, better productivity, and efficient leadership.

We now know what it takes to draft a talent mobility program for the organization. This would obviously allow you to structure the program well but there are greater details that go into the planning phase that allow you to tailor the program properly according to the specific requirements of your organization.

These details are unique for every organization and that is why it is difficult to discuss each one of them here in this book. However, all these details stem from the organizational facts and it is hence you need to know why these facts are so important for the talent mobility programs to be formulated right.

We previously did mention the importance of getting the facts right before making the move. We cannot stress it enough. Most organizations allow their mobility programs to be governed by unknowns. *Does that help them?* NO it doesn't!

It may seem like they are saving time in the short-run which appears as an advantage to most but since the impact of talent mobility does not become evident in short time spans it is difficult to judge the complete effect of the whole move until it's too late – obviously the time when the losses become apparent and the temporary turbulence takes form of a full- force disaster.

Often collecting factual data wouldn't require you to look beyond the organization's human resource department. These departments have more than half of the relevant data available in their systems. The remaining facts can be obtained from the data relating to the overall business performance and the financial data available to allow the management to take well informed and calculated mobility decisions.

These facts can be used to determine the current standing of talent mobility in the organization, assess the overall impact of this mobility, and help shape the mobility program for the future.

When we say the data/these facts help the organization determine the current standing of talent mobility in the organization, here's what we are referring to:

These facts help you understand the role of mobility in your organization. You need to acknowledge the fact that talent mobility is a form of investment that companies make in their employees. If this investment does not generate a viable return for the company it's only wasting the resources. Hence, unless talent mobility is playing a substantial role in the   progress of the organization, it may not be something you need to invest your resources in.

This data can help you determine what employee has worked on which positions and the duration they spent on that position. In addition to that, you can obtain a summary of the estimated costs the organization incurs with every rotation in terms of money, time, and lost productivity. It can even assist you in breaking down the current policy into workforce segments, geographical positioning, and business functions for a comprehensive insight of the current policy and its workings. This is especially helpful when you are trying to assess the overall impact and performance of the policy.

Mobility brings a series of consequences that range between the good and the bad. These consequences have their due effect on both the organization and its employees. We discussed how effective talent mobility policies resulted in an overall positive impact on the performance and retention of employees in Marriott International. If you look at ways in which individuals benefit from mobility, you need to count things like career growth, increase in remunerations, longer retention periods, high level of engagement, and continuous learning.

When it comes to assessing the impact of the talent mobility policies on the business as a whole, the deal is pretty simple – you could simply take a look at the performance of the business for that particular period. Financial statements, quality control information, market performance, and other relevant statistic can help you gauge the impact of the policy you implemented during the period in question.

When you're able to size up the positive and negative aspects of your current mobility policy you get a clear vision of the direction you wish to take your next policy in and the objectives you wish to achieve through it. It gives you a chance to size up the irregularities in the current policies and make amends to them so that you can avoid the same fall outs for the future. It also allows you to determine which employees would be best suited for your next talent mobility program and how you can hone and shape their capabilities for future leadership.

We've gone on and on about the importance of talent mobility policies and the benefits they can bring to the organization. We have also pointed out the places that require special attention in case organizations are aiming for a well-rounded talent mobility program that reaps actual measurable benefits for them. Again, for the policy to work and the plan to take effect you need a set of strategies that can help you make the most of your talent management program or improve the one that is already in place.

So what strategies can you implement to make sure your talent mobility program becomes an efficient tool for leadership development and talent retention in the organization?

HOW TO IMPROVE TALENT MOBILITY WITHIN THE ORGANIZATION?

When designing strategies for improving the talent mobility structure in your organization, in addition to the things we discussed above, you need to make sure your employees see a future for their career with your organization. Your strategies should be focused on providing maximum opportunity to your employees for them to grow as professionals and as individuals as their career progresses through the years to accomplish the career aspirations they set for themselves. They also need to acknowledge that the organization is contributing to their pursuit of self-actualization by giving them a chance to enhance their knowledge, improve their skills, and enrich their experiences that add up to creating job satisfaction for them – which for the company means, active employee engagement, higher employee retention, better productivity, and an overall improved performance.

Isn't that a win-win scenario for you and your organization?

IT ALL BEGINS WITH THE GOALS

Whether you like it or not, we're here discussing goals again. Only this time it is not the individual goals that we would be focusing on. Rather, this time we want you to think about the objectives that you wish to accomplish with the implementation of a proper talent mobility program. Remember, if you do not have substantial goals that you want to set and achieve, it is pointless to tie up your resources into a talent management program with no intended output.

The most important thing at this point is to have a vision. That vision allows you to set goals that your mobility program can address. These goals could be improving the employee turnover or achieving high employee engagement scores. Make sure you set no more than two goals at a time. These should be precise and clearly defined for anyone who wishes to understand the objectives behind them.

Once you're done with the setting of goals, the next step is to define the parameters that will be used to track the effectiveness of the program as it sets its course to achieve the said targets. Your gauge metrics need to be uniform throughout the different levels of the mobility program to ensure proper analysis and data that can be followed through to measure the success or failure of the policy.

MAKE IT TRANSPARENT

There is no point to implementing a program or policy if the ones it is actually meant for (the employees) are potentially unaware of it. As soon as you lay out the particulars of a policy, the first thing you should do is address the relevant employees *(top talent in case of sponsored mobility and all employees in a contest mobility scenario)* and tell them everything there is to know about the mobility program.

This may include a briefing on how the program is supposed to work and the parameters it will operate by. It is also important to clarify the employee selection criteria that will be used to pick relevant employees from the lot for leadership development. Another crucial aspect that should be highlighted is the goals that the organization wants to accomplish with this policy in action and the recognition and rewards that would be bestowed upon the deserving employees (if any).

Since we have already discussed a lot about transparency when we talked about active people engagement (APE), it is clear that employees appreciate being made privy to the "other greater details" related to managerial decisions. Hence, you need to keep them updated about the latest developments in the policy and any other changes related to it that may impact the performance and engagement level of the employees.

KEEP AN EYE OUT FOR HIGH POTENTIAL EMPLOYEES

While it's a good initiative to work on developing every single employee in the organization, it often doesn't payback well. This is mostly because not everyone possesses the tendencies, will, and capability to grow and improve. Sometimes, even people who have the capabilities and potential to grow lack the earnest willpower that drives them to the path of sustained success.

It is therefore important for the organization to carefully select the people it wants to spend time and money on. See, if this employee that you spend time training and developing does not want to achieve the level of progress that you wish to see him on – there is nothing in there for the organization. So in order to make talent mobility work best you need to pick employees that have the aspiration, the ability, the values, and most importantly the commitment to grow while remaining in the same organization – your organization.

This obviously makes a cut for the nomads – ones who are always looking for an opportunity to switch jobs, trying one thing after another – millennials? Probably, but not all of them. Like we mentioned earlier that even though the millennials quickly get bored of monotonous work routine or something that is not of interest to them not all of them may be able to afford quitting the job. Some may even enjoy their present work or like the work environment enough to stick around in the organization longer than predicted. You've got to find that inner drive that can be exploited with the talent mobility program to have employees aiming higher in terms of growth and progress. You have to find a way to unleash the leader that is sleeping inside of them.

Besides talent mobility is a great opportunity for employees to learn more than they know. It allows them to enhance their skill and knowledge pool. It will always work with employees who have the thirst to experience more than their current position allows them to. Keeping this in mind, the best source of determining which employees to shortlist for targeted leadership development is the one-on-one sessions with employees that can help the management get an idea of what exactly the employee needs to push him for actively pursuing career growth.

THE CULTURE IS IMPORTANT TOO

When we discussed Marriott International and their policy of talent mobility, it was clearly evident that mobility of employees is deeply embedded in the culture of this organization. Each employee recruited into the organization KNOWS for a fact that there will be a time they will be mobilized to obtain leadership succession goals or other relevant objectives of the business.

There's no surprise to it. They are aware that as and when required, these employees may be asked to fill in a different post in the same or a different business unit for the organization. When you make it a part of the organizational culture, the employees that are inducted and the ones already working would be attuned to the process of learning and career transitioning through multiple rotations, continuous coaching, and valuable mentoring.

It makes the implementation and execution of the mobility relevant policies easier for the management. Normally, talent mobility implementation may bring unwanted disruption in the processes of the business as employees take time to accept, adjust to, and get familiar with the new policies and their aftermath. Since it is widely acceptable as the organization's culture, there is little chance that it might create chaos or give rise to criticism from the employees in general.

People tend to get better accustomed to things they are already expecting to happen. This is where a mobility culture in the organization can help you make the most of the process and its goals.

BRING IN DIVERSITY

For most employees, career growth is signified by a move that levels them up on the organizational chart. Generally, if you ask a potential sales candidate where they'd like to see themselves in the organization 5 years down the line, the answer would probably be *"heading the regional sales team that I'm being hired for at the moment."* That's the vision most employees have for their career aspirations and it's not entirely wrong.

However, if you look at it this way: You currently have 5 sales executives working in the regional sales team under one regional manager. Three out of these executives are extremely talented and have time and again shown extempore leadership skills in various tasks and projects. Now when you ask these three executives what their career aspirations are, you would most likely get the same answer we discussed above. This is where the problem lies. You do have the talent that can be developed to fill in the shoes of the current regional manager in the future, but do you have enough regional sales management positions to accommodate the career goals of all three of them?

At this point you may want to look into the other regional sales teams of the organization, but then even they have talented individuals in line to succeed the position. And when they get to know that they can't have their desired growth in this organization, they'll start looking for others that may offer them a better chance at it. *So what do you do? How do you make it work?*

You go back to step one. Dig deeper into the individual skills and potential of each of these talents. Look for alternate business functions and operational areas where these individuals can put their secondary skills to use. You mobilize these employees, see where they fit best. Now it is important at this stage to inform your employees why you took these steps. Add a new horizon to their vision. Let them know that despite being good at sales, they have the capability to excel equally or sometimes even more in another function of the business, let's say marketing or the administrative aspects of sales and marketing.

When you're at it, you need to take a smart approach to the process. Sometimes it wouldn't be easy to convince these employees. At times you may even see them leaving the organization for what they perceive is a better opportunity for them, but you need to stay put and employ your salesmanship to sell this idea to the employees. You need to show them that "UP" is not the only direction on the organizational chart that they can aim for. With businesses becoming increasingly multidimensional these days the organizations are now being defined by flatter organizational charts that consequently brings more chances of cross-functional collaboration on different levels.

Moving in a different direction altogether could be daunting for employees, and encouragement alone would not be able to suffice for the support and assurance they need to move ahead from here. So you need to work in a little bit of added motivation.

You're asking an employee to leave their long planned goals for something that appeared completely out of the blue for them. Not everybody is okay with taking risks of that caliber.

While there may be some employees who dive into a new opportunity without giving it a second thought, most will carefully evaluate the pros and cons of the situation. To make things go your way, you should make sure the pros are way more than the perceivable cons. This is where your pay grades will come in handy.

Where in most cases monetary compensation or incentives aren't as effective as other motivational factors to drive the employees into giving their professional best; here, at this point, it is exactly what you need to sway them into heading forward in a career direction you've planned for them. Therefore, the sensible way forward is to support your internal mobility plans with a proper pay grade system that is compensating and motivating enough for the employees to consider a career path switch.

Diversity is healthy and you need to be able to make your employees understand how internal rotation or external mobility can help them enrich their careers and it chances for sustained growth. Also, this is a good time to discuss the pool of skills and capabilities possessed by these employees on an individual basis and help them see how their abilities can allow them to shine at a position/place different than that of their choosing. Once these employees acknowledge the fact that this mobility program is designed to add value to their careers and help them accomplish their goals *(slightly differently than they had planned)*, they are most likely to stick around and give this multi- directional career transition a shot.

FOCUS ON THE LEARNING

Smart entrepreneurs have this unique ability of far-sightedness. They can see where the organization given its current resources is headed to; and predict what resources the organization would further need in order to achieve its planned long-term goals. This entrepreneurial approach is expected from the management when it comes to making talent mobility an effective approach for leadership development.

Leadership development is a comprehensive process that may take years to bear fruit. However, over these years if this process is not provided with the adequate amounts of training, experiences, opportunities, and coaching, it may just wither mid-way. It's just like a plant that wilts if it does not get the required amount of water and sunlight to complete the process of photosynthesis.

The point here is, that no matter what talent mobility program you introduce or are in the process of introducing, you need to bring your employees to a level where they can take up the new challenges posed by their mobilization. This is where the learning comes into play. It needs to be focused. It needs to be in just the right amount at the right time. Let's continue with our previous example of the three talented sales executives and see how this works.

After taking a close look at each of these three individuals, you discover that one of them

(A) is good with the administrative work related to sale. (A) possesses all the required skills: he is organized, he is quick, he is well-versed with documentation and filing processes of the business and has a flair for inter department liaising. Therefore, you decide to place his first rotation into the Human Resource department where he can employ both his administrative and sales-related skills to help the HR department perform better and more efficiently.

Since sales and HR are two functions that have almost nothing in common, it might not be easy for (A) to pick up his new job responsibilities and start performing them to the best of his abilities as soon as he is transferred. It would leave him completely bamboozled and may hamper the efficient performance of both departments (sales and HR).

Now how do you stop that from happening?

You prepare him and the departments for the switch. This may include making place for an additional person in the HR function and distributing the jobs of (A) among the remaining sales executives in the team (in case there is no temporary replacement). But above all that, it will include the basic training and mentoring required to help (A) know his way around how things work in the HR department, who he is supposed to report to, how will he be expected to work, and the basic terminologies of the department that he might need to get familiarized with.

In short, you need to gear (A) up for his new job description and surroundings. Instead of burdening him with loads of knowledge, tips, and trainings, try and focus only on polishing the relevant skills they require to complete their new responsibilities. This will make your employees more flexible and adaptive for the new department and help them ease into it better. The lesser time they take to settle the sooner the company gets to reap the benefits.

You as the organization leader/manager can take the initiative to play around with these strategies and tweak them accordingly so that they fit better into your organization's respective environment. However, you need to realize that talent management on the whole is much larger than any of the above mentioned tools on their own. Active people engagement (APE), encouraged intrapreneurship, and talent mobility form only part of the greater picture. All of these elements need to be combined together and formed into a program that can collectively deal with the acquisition, retention, and development of talent within the organization.

Previously, we also studied the concept of individual tailored needs (ITN) and how organizations can utilize their skills inventory efficiently with the implementation of integrated talent management systems. What we didn't mention back then however, is the fact that that APE, intrapreneurship, and talent mobility are active elements of an integrated talent management program that work together to create a robust system of talent management that can bring around the positivity a business requires to outperform the cut-throat competition in the industry in order to survive.

We started this book with the agenda to learn how organizations can cope with the challenge of managing and retaining the new generation of talent – the corporate nomads – the millennials. They are unique in their ways and set in their principles but so are most organizations. *In this war between modern day organizations and the millennials who would emerge as the victor?*

Truth is it's the organization that stands to lose the most. You may feel the need to ask: *why or how?*

As much as the experts have understood the millennial way of life, if there is anything at all that they actually care about – it's themselves. If they want the society to be a better place – you know, free of poverty and hunger or the latest social developments like

#BlackLivesMatter and *#GayPride* - it's because they themselves do not want to live amid the harsh realities that often go unnoticed. We're not saying that these youngsters lack compassion or are too selfish to care about anything else at all – but when it comes to organizations, this breed of professionals want to keep their interests before the organization's interests as their priority.

Come to think of it, it's not really difficult to understand the workings of a millennial mind. The one thing that you shouldn't forget is that these employees are young – *young and impulsive!* They do not have the habit of thinking through before taking a decision. If there is something they want, they'll go ahead (work for it) and get it and if they realize they can't get it from you, they find someone else who could give them the same. Recall the time when you were young – *weren't you as impetuous as the millennials?* Maybe not when it came to your job, but for everything else it was pretty much the same.

The important thing to notice here is the fact that these millennials, contrary to the popular belief that labels them as lazy, are ready to work for what they want. And that is where you need to exploit them. You give them what they want and they'll stick around with you for longer. Everybody is selfish and it's all about give and take – you give some, you gain some.

It's actually THAT simple.

If it were this simple, why do you think we took the pain to compile a 200+ page book to provide a solution for this problem? It's because often the simplest of solutions are overlooked by organizations in an attempt to overcome issues that are only an extension of what they have faced time and over again. Obviously, every generation entered the corporate world with their own unique set of beliefs, principles, and character traits that came to define them as a group; but organizations managed to overcome these challenges with adequate strategies and effective planning of resources.

In the beginning, we listed down a series of expectations that millennials have from the organizations they work for. These included:

- Continuous Learning

- Flexible Schedules

- Greater Good

From the looks of it, this isn't much they're asking for in return for the plethora of talent and creativity they could bestow on the organization. One can't deny that this generation is more educated and more tech savvy than any other generations that preceded them. They have been born and brought up in a fast-paced world where people usually do not have the time to wait outside the manager's room until they're called in for an audience; they'd rather just text their way out of a situation and call it a legit communication channel. Given that, in actual it is not just the three things listed above that they expect from their organization – they WANT a complete makeover of the corporate culture. *See how that links to the title of this book?*

Millennials want to redefine the conventional organizations to suit their quick and agile lifestyle. The smarter organizations have already set pace for this paradigm shift and are making the move as and when they can, but it hasn't happened overnight. This process has taken years – considering the first millennials entered the corporate world almost two decades ago – the far-sighted entrepreneurs began the evolution back then. Today if corporate giants like Google and Microsoft are efficiently managing their young lot of employees, it's because they have worked years over to create a system that gives these millennials an environment where they can be themselves that is young, enthusiastic, and creative.

Good thing is, it's not too late. Well the youngest millennials are still 12 years old and will be entering the job market in about a minimum 6 of 8 years. That gives you almost a decade to make the necessary changes to the processes and culture of the organization so that it is better equipped to deal appropriately with these corporate rebels. And here's the plus point, Generation Z will not be much different from Generation Y. This means that the changes you make will be reaping long term benefits and establishing an organizational culture that the younger lot can relate to.

This book was focused on how proper talent management can prove to be a useful tool for the organization in reaching this objective of creating a millennial-friendly work environment. Now changing the organizational culture altogether is subject to a flurry of hurdles that make it an extremely challenging task to be completed in the short run, but talent management can give you the start you need to set pace.

When we talk about talent management, we are actually addressing the biggest problem faced by organizations these days in managing millennial talent – the low retention rates. When employees don't stick around for long in an organization there are multiple adverse consequences that the organization faces as an aftermath. These may include some or all of the following:

THE TALENT DRAIN

This is one of the most obvious repercussions of high employee turnover in the organization. When employees keep leaving the organization every now and then they cause continuous fluctuations in the talent pool of the organization; and although it is important for organizations to update their skills inventory on a regular basis, doing so every week because someone left and another joined the organization is quite impractical. It leads to confusion and at times may even cause the management to overlook the relevant talent that is already present in the skills inventory or the one the organization lacks and needs to acquire. This could prove disastrous given the fast-paced competitive environments most organizations compete in.

Besides that, losing key talent means there will be an obvious loss in the productivity of the organization, let alone the processes that may experience lack of efficiency or required skills to be managed efficiently.

THE INCREASE IN COSTS

When employees leave, they have to be replaced. This may seem like one of the most natural processes of the corporate world, but it comes with a cost. The recruitment process and training programs require time, effort, and money to be put in action. The same time, effort, and money could be invested somewhere else in the business that could bring high potential returns to the organization. Hence we are not just talking about a loss in finances and productivity; we have to consider the opportunity cost attached to the process as well. When added, these costs can become a significant amount that can wreak considerable havoc on the business and its operations.

THE DISTRACTIONS

High employee turnover in the organization tends to distract the management, other employees, and the organization as a whole from the real objectives of the business. Decision making in an organization is highly contingent to the corporate vision its management has for it. When employees frequently leave the organization, it distracts the operations and decision making process of the business away from the corporate vision they set out to achieve. A high employee turnover tends to have a dual impact on the business and its operations.

When current employees leave, they push the organization backwards on the road to achieving the corporate goals it has and when a new batch of employees is hired to fill the shoes of the ones that left, it's more like the organization is back to square one. The entire process has to start from the scratch or from very near to the starting line in the very least.

LOSING THE COMPETITIVE EDGE

There are no two thoughts over the fact that an organization's employees are its greatest asset. They bring in the necessary talent – skills, experience, knowledge, and expertise – the organization requires to accomplish its long and short-term targets. This very talent is also something that gives the organization a competitive edge over other organizations operating in the same market and/or industry.

For organizations that experience high employee turnover this competitive edge lacks the strength to help the organization outperform its competition. The right talent in the right place at the right time means productive efficiency – low costs, high outputs. And in an attempt to acquire this productive efficiency, most organizations invest time and money in to strategic programs aimed at honing their employees' skills for maximum output.

With a regular influx of new employees, it becomes imperative to conduct continuous training sessions to bring them up to a level where their contributions to the business are meaningful and adequate for the company's collective goals. If organizations don't do that, they will lose out any competitive edge that they have or have the potential to achieve over their competition.

Plus, there is additional bad news: The employees that leave your organization may look for or take up jobs in a similar organization and most likely in the same industry – your competition!

High employee turnover is not healthy for organizations on the whole. It's a cancer that gradually weakens the organization from the inside – something that will eventually lead to a downfall. So when the millennials leave your organization, they are brick by brick taking you down and that needs to stop. The only way about it is to bring a cultural change in the organization but that cannot happen overnight.

So it's better to start with something that in the least convinces your millennial employees that staying in the organization will prove more beneficial for their career and the aspirations they have attached to it. A ROBUST TALENT MANAGEMENT PROGRAM IS WHAT YOU NEED.

Talent management may not be the complete solution to the millennial dilemma of the organizations but it could be used to hold on to unique talent long enough to make them realize that the organization is working towards creating the exact work environment they want and need to thrive in it. If we rationally look at the situation, it is clear that every organization would be out to get their hands on the best talent available within their reach

– *why would anyone settle for anything less?*

What organizations need to realize is the fact that recruiting the best talent given their limited resources is only the beginning. The real deal begins once the talent acquired becomes a part of the caravan moving to the end destination. See the talent you acquire, especially when we're talking about the millennials, it's raw and fresh. These people have just transitioned from a laidback college life to a systematic professional life. They have the passion, they have the skills, they may lack the experience but they do have the knowledge.

What they need at this point is a direction, a guidance that helps them channel their talent in a way that it adds value to the organization and its goals. So your talent management program basically needs to address every single thing that allows these youngsters to use their maximum potential and grow as individuals and professionals with the very organization they work for.

COMBINING THE ELEMENTS OF TALENT MANAGEMENT

Each element of talent management that we have discussed throughout the course of this book has its own relevant significance for the effective talent management of employees – we say "employees" and not just millennials because devising a talent management program only for the millennials will only brew up further trouble in the organization as other generations of employees in the workforce feel left out.

First things first, you need a talent management strategy designed to properly acquire, develop, and place talent within the organization. These strategies need to be aligned to the goals of the company; they should lay down a clear outline of the development opportunities created through various company initiatives, should have well-defined metrics to gauge their success and monitor employee growth, and should be supported by a formal recognition and reward policy that dictates the appraisals of these employees.

Now you obviously can't have the talent management program with no talent to manage. This brings us to defining strategies that direct organizations into hiring and retaining required talent in the organization. You need to have a clear plan as to who you recruit and what are your priorities for short-listing candidates. It's all right if these priorities focus on qualification and experiences and relevance – *but if you're smart you'll take the road less travelled and pick employees that display creativity in their thoughts and ideas.*

Why do we suggest that? Because creativity cannot be instilled - you cannot put innovative ideas into someone's mind to make them think that way or alter their perception about things according to it. Even if you could manage that, it would take years for that person to mold into that particular thought process and you're already short on time. On the contrary, hiring a person who already has the ability to think outside the box will only require you to identify what they're best at, polish them and their skills up, and place them where they are most needed to bring success to the organization.

With the recruitment process dealt, your next step in developing a sound talent management program is to focus on the talent present in the organization. You have an inventory of diverse skills in the form of your employees and most of them would be in place where required. However, it is unlikely that the talent pool you possess is fulfilling all the talent requirements of the organization. Instead of looking for recruiting new talent, it is better to give first preference to the employees already in the organization.

We know that you hired them for specific roles and purposes, but *have you ever pondered upon the possibility that the employees working in one position can actually be a better fit for another position in a completely different function of the organization?* Gone are the days when your qualification decided which department of the organization you will be serving in and the millennials on the whole, are completely defying the unsaid law of spending an eternity in the same organization doing the same job over and over.

This brings in the concept of talent mobility to be combined in effect with the working strategies of the talent management program as an effective tool for enriching and developing employees for roles other than what they were hired for. And for the talent mobility process to be successful you need a specialized team (internally formed or external) who is familiar with the psyche and thinking patterns of each employee and can appropriately analyze them in context to the organizational talent requirements.

The safest way out of this one happens to be focusing only on the core talent in the company. Employees who time and over exhibit solid potential of excelling in highly diverse roles and have the leadership abilities to carry their skills all the way in giving the optimal level of productivity and when in leadership positions encouraging others to do the same.

Could you guess what impact the above mentioned scenario would have on the millennials?

If you recall back to the first few chapters of the book, we mentioned how the millennials are looking for quick growth and diversity in their work. They appreciate continuous learning and want to regularly add to their knowledge, skills, and expertise. They also want their jobs to have a creative element that allows them to employ their innovative thought processes to their everyday jobs. *Isn't all that provided by talent mobility?*

Well obviously something needs to be done about enhancing the creativity element in there. *Don't you think?* So we go ahead and add the encouraged intrapreneurship policy into the talent management program already supported by a strategy for talent mobility. This would obviously require you to make certain changes to the corporate environment in your organization. It would mean that the managers have to largely alter their management styles. The incorporation of intrapreneurship-relevant strategies may even be met with hostility by the other generation of employees but you need to be able to play to your strengths.

Rope in the loyal employees first. Make them understand how this creative environment can actually help the *"organization"* grow. It'll work sure shot for the boomers. The Gen X may be a little trickier to deal with.

Simply because there would be a difference of opinion among them; while the creative ones may see the policies as a chance to bring forth their ideas and innovation and have greater control of the tasks at hand, others may be skeptical of the organization's real motive behind the move.

You need to keep in mind that any change in the organizational culture, no matter how small would cause controversy. The management in this case needs to be strong enough to control the adverse reactions and transition them into positive outlooks for the employees and the organization as a whole.

In essence, bringing a cultural change in the organization is highly dependent on the way the management channels themselves into the modern ways of administering the talent available in the organization. It is the management that the employees look up to for proper leadership and guidance, and hence it is the management that needs to initiate the process of change. Most people in management positions consider change to be nothing more than an unnecessary distraction from the set curriculum of the work culture, but they fail to realize that it is change that determines progress.

"One key to successful leadership is continuous personal change. Personal change is a reflection of our inner growth and empowerment." — Robert E. Quinn

Change is what drives the organization to the road of sustained success. Had the managements of Google, Marriott, and Microsoft not made constant relevant changes over the years to their work culture, *do you think they would have been able to have the corporate standing that they enjoy today?*

Modern managements need to realize the real worth of their position in the organization. They have the ability to make or break the future of the organization, simply because the employees follow course depending on how the management conduct themselves. It is therefore imperative that the recruitment process for managerial positions is dealt with extreme caution.

There are generally two ways a company looks to fill a managerial position. One, it can look for potential candidates within the organization; two, it could set an external recruitment process in motion. Regardless of the channel an organization chooses to deal with this matter, they need proper strategies in place to make sure the candidate selected is one that can lead from the front and add value to the organization and its goals.

Since encouraged intrapreneurship requires establishing a creative working atmosphere in the organization, a manager who is too set in their ways to allow the "chaos" of creativity in the system will never be able to mold themselves into someone who encourages employees to take risks or to be innovative with their ideas and work styles. Like we said, creativity cannot be instilled. *So what can you do about it?*

Instead of venturing out to look for possible managers that can bring a positive burst of innovation and creativity to the work environment, most organizations focus on building succession plans for existing employees. See hiring a new manager may not be an issue for most organizations, but the story doesn't end there – it only just begins. A new manager would obviously bring in external expertise and fresh ideas to the company, but there is always the chance that they'd have a difficult time settling down in the new environment or in some cases are not well-accepted by their subordinates.

Adequate career succession plans can help organizations overcome this shortcoming of hiring external managers. A succession plan is an important element of efficient talent management in the organization. It basically helps you map out a future career progress plan for the existing employees. Smart organizations include their employees in the process of drafting career succession plans, making sure the plans encompass the individual career aspirations of the employees in them.

Take a look back to our initial example of the three sales executives who wished to progress through five years of their time in the organization to land the position of the regional sales manager. All three of them have the capability and talent to progress to that position. However, during your individual sessions with each one of them you realize that (C) exhibits exceptional leadership skills whenever placed in a team scenario.

Also, he has a creative knack in him that allows him to look at things from a different perspective and convince others on the basis of facts and expertise over matters concerning utmost attention of the department as a whole.

An ordinary manager would see an extremely talented employee who is driven by the passion to excel in everything that he does. On the other hand, a smart manager would see a potential manager in (C), one who is capable of combining the elements of strong leadership and creative style of working into a potent persona that fits just right for modern day leadership in organizations. Coming back to our point, it is these employees – the ones like (C) that organizations need to work upon to develop themselves for their future roles in the company.

While a succession plan for (C) would be focused on equipping him with the necessary knowledge, training, mentoring, and skills required to run as a forefront manager; there will be other succession plans drawn for the remaining two executives that take their individual capabilities into consideration before deciding an internal career path for them. What you're practicing at this moment is the concept of individual tailored needs (ITN). We've discussed it earlier in the book in greater depth to make you understand the impact this concept can have on the overall efficiency of the organization.

For talent management to be successful, it is necessary that each step of the way from recruitment to retention is adequately covered with effective strategies that help the organization gradually transition into the culture it wishes to achieve. When we talk about introducing a culture of innovation and creativity, you need to begin TODAY.

How? Follow the three basic elements: recruit, encourage, reward.

You need to recruit creative people, encourage their creativity, and adequately reward it to set the game in motion. However, before all that make sure your current management is open to change and strong enough to deal with the disruption that might be caused with the sudden influx of creativity in the organization. To date, you have been focusing on hiring the right candidate for the right job. Now, you need to add the element of creativity to the equation as well. So ideally, your strategy should be to hire the right candidate, who has the creative ability to excel in the right position.

When you bring in new employees, a majority of which would be millennials unless you're hiring for positions other than the ones on the entry level, you bring in a fresh set of expertise, knowledge, skills, and abilities to the organization. Top that with the added element of creativity and you have a complete package that you can nourish and develop to take control of the organizations reins in the future.

This change in strategy that will now determine the hiring policies of the company will ensure that the new breed of employees entering the organization have talent supported by adequate creativity that gives them a competitive edge over other employees in the company. When these new employees settle into the new environment and begin employing their creativity and innovative ideas into every task assigned to them, they may help others explore their own creative sides. They may inspire other employees to look for better ways of accomplishing the same targets making processes simple and less time consuming.

The fact that even the most creative employees cannot flourish as much as they should unless they are provided an environment that allows them to grow has been already established in this book. When it comes to who will establish this environment? The answer is simple – the management. It is the management that will lead the change; it is the management that needs to take a step towards introducing working policies that liberate the employees enough to take certain job-related decisions and exercise control over their projects – this counts into the 'encouragement of creativity' we just mentioned a while ago. It will automatically bring transparency in the work processes as employees take the initiative to collaborate and focus on the things that matter most to their career advancements and the collective progress of the organization.

The next and the most crucial factor that can actually motivate most employees into taking the innovative approach to their assigned jobs is the proper system of recognition and rewards for the creative ones. Again, you as the management need to be aware of the fact that not everyone in the workforce would be motivated by monetary rewards. At this point, it would be a smart decision to again work the concept of ITN into the process, determine what drives each of the employees in question and design adequate reward strategies to make sure every employee gives in their best input to contribute to the overall productivity of the organization.

A change of culture in the organization would affect the level of engagement in the organization. Like we pointed out earlier, some may take the change as a potential opportunity to show the organization and the management what exactly they're made of; others would have a negative outlook on the entire scenario. It's all about the employees' perception – the way they see and analyze things happening around them. In a situation as such, you would feel the need to incorporate the 4 principles of APE into the whole talent management program that helps you improve the level of active engagement employees practice on their jobs.

Over the course of this chapter we have been discussing everything that we've read throughout the book. We have been trying to connect the dots between the various concepts of talent management that in one way or another greatly contribute to the success or failure of the talent management program within an organization. The talent management program is not just relevant for getting the best out of the available human capital in the business. It is more about making sure that the new generation of employees gets a proper environment that can help them grow as individuals and professionals in addition to making them realize their true capabilities and the massive improvements they can bring within the organization making use of that potential.

Many a times, in an attempt to design and implement a proper talent management system in the organizations, managements push limits to get the necessary done so that they can have an efficient system to employ, nurture, and enhance the skills, knowledge, and expertise of their employees. In pursuit of getting everything right there is one extremely important element that they often overlook – technology.

Yes, we have been going over and over the fact that organizations need a cultural change, managers need to alter their management styles, employees' creativity need to be promoted and so on. But at the end of the day, to be able to manage all of that manually is going to require a miracle! No matter how many hands your human resource department has got on board, and how efficiently the responsibilities have been divided within the team members; the talent management program will fall apart if the strategies do not have a platform to culminate into one robust program for the proper administration of the process.

Consider an example. Your organization employs 50 employees in total. The human resource management department currently has two members in the team who deal with everything related to hiring, firing, promotions, rewards and recognitions, skills inventory management, keeping track of employee attendance, conducting training and learning programs, monitoring employee growth and helping departmental managers maintain employee portfolios that help determine which employee should be a part of the leadership development programs, and conducting regular sessions with employees to upgrade their manual database for the individual tailored needs of each employee.

These 2 people divide the administrative and the human capital management elements equally between each other, but there is always a fall out at one place or another. Both employees HR1 and HR2 are professionals and know their jobs well. They have kept all the records and have been efficiently taking care of all the human resource-related matters of the company – but individually. HR1 has everything on his part of the jobs done and completed just the same as HR2 – they both can provide relevant data and details related to what they individually handle - *then what could be the possible fall out?*

The problem arises where they have to collectively answer about two or more task/HR functions that are interconnected but performed by them separately. For example, HR1 is responsible for updating the skills inventory and it is HR2 who makes the workforce plan in collaboration with the other department heads. They both have the relevant details required to sum up both these databases, but when they are asked to link the two they find out there are certain bits of information that each had missed simply because that part wasn't in their job description.

This example portrays the very basic level of this problem. As organizations grow in size and operations their human resource functions become more complicated and while hiring new people in the department may seem like a good solution – *it's not!* What you need instead is a proper system – a software that amalgamates all of these functions into one solid program that can be accessed across the board in the organization and take the notion of transparency to an entirely different level – one that would definitely gain the millennial fandom.

You need an integrated talent management system. Talent management is redefining the modern day human resource management function and pairing it with technology will only make you move towards your organizational goals a lot quicker than you originally were.

Consider our HR1 and HR2 example again. At first these two HR personnel maintained individual records of their assigned tasks and had trouble connecting the two when required. With the integrated talent management system in place, they would continue their jobs the same way – the only difference would be that the lost connection would be automatically created by the software. This type of software is programmed to connect the A, B, C and so on of your talent management program that creates a strong framework for your talent management strategies to be more effective than they are without it. With a proper structure defined for how the program works and what it takes to put something specific into implementation, everyone throughout the organization is aware of what they should and shouldn't do to make the most of the talent management strategy of the company.

It brings the employees and the management on the same page. Everyone is aware of how the system works, and what can they get out of it. The idea is to eliminate the need for running up to the human resource department to know how the company rewards achievements and performance of their employees or which employees can be considered for the upcoming talent mobility program.

For the management this becomes a resourceful database that can be looked into to judge the performance of an employee or keep track of an internee who has the potential to make a great executive for the organization and enjoy a thriving career in the same – there could be various uses. For the employees, an integrated talent management system can help track their progress and map their professional journey in the company. They can stay updated with the learning and training initiatives introduced by the company to help them develop their skills and make the most of the opportunities provided to them to make it where they want to be professionally.

The point is that we could go on and on about how the integrated talent management software can revolutionize the talent management process in the organization. It is one of the most overlooked wonder of technology that can actually transform the culture of an organization without much chaos – yes, the same culture we have been talking about throughout this chapter – the culture that the millennials can be at peace with.

So the question is:

Is it really the millennials that are redefining the talent and human capital management in modern day organizations?

You could credit them with the fact that they're actually the ones that have made organizations consider the fact that there is something missing in the way they manage business and its operations that is not sitting well with this latest breed of employees. Part of it is obviously because the millennials are different. They want what they want and they wouldn't settle for anything less than that. This fact about them has made organizational managements stay the nights up looking for plausible solutions that can help them get past this dilemma.

Many managers resist the change, thinking that if they give in to one demand of the millennials, these youngsters will pile up a heap of other demands that would be required to be fulfilled to make them work. What these managers fail to consider is the fact that even though the millennials go overboard with their list of demands – transparency, growth, flexibility, purpose, autonomy, etc.–most of these requests are pretty much the need of the hour for modern day organizations.

Truth is, the baby boomers would soon retire. The Gen X would be taking up the managerial positions but they lack the creativity required to stay abreast the rapidly changing corporate environment in different industries. At this point, if you can prepare and promote the millennials to a level where they if not take the managerial position can provide good competition to the Gen X employees forcing them to bring out the best of their creativity – you are still winning on the whole.

In the alternate scenario, if you develop the same millennials for future leadership and have them success the key managerial positions currently help by the boomers (in most cases), you as the organization are still at an advantage. None of us disagrees on the fact that the millennials are far more educated and tech savvy than the Gen X or the Boomers. They have seen the best of both worlds; and even though their way of working is rather unconventional for the old-school batch of business gurus, they do possess the ability to change the course of the organizations performance.

As far as this book is concerned, we have tried our best to help modern entrepreneurs, leaders, and managers understand the prevailing situation of the corporate environment at this point in time. We're standing here in 2016, at a point where the proliferation of technology has fast tracked every possible thing in the world. The corporate world took the impact too – a rather strong one.

In the past corporations that competed in the same industry had to rely heavily on operational and natural elements to gain a competitive advantage over others in the industry. Never before the corporate environment saw the focus of businesses centered on their employees. However, things have taken a drastic turn today. It is the employees that are steering modern day organizations towards the successful accomplishment of their goals and the same organizations are being forced to recognize the importance of their employees. And part of this recognition has been instilled by the millennials!

The process of human capital management in organizations has always been in the need for a complete makeover. It is only now that managements in different organizations are actually opening their eyes and minds to the fact that they require a set of plausible working strategies that can pull the system together for better efficiency – now that they are having a hard time dealing with and accommodating the free-willed strong-headed millennials.

Hence, to say that the millennials are redefining the human capital management norms in modern day organizations may be justified to an extent. Take the real life example in this case. Living our lives, we often feel that everything is exactly how it should be; that our circumstances and way of living is as good as it could and should be. However, as life goes on we sometimes come across situations or scenarios that act as eye-openers for us. They make us realize that not everything in our life was as it should have been; that there was something missing, something that required our attention for the longest of time.

This usually happens because we as individuals become accustomed to the way things are and we make an effort to mold our way of life accordingly. Corporate organizations face similar circumstances. They have been following a set pattern of processes and work patterns that they rarely realize there is something that needs their immediate attention – in this case it's the human capital management. When the millennials entered, the same organizations saw their active employee engagement scores and employee retention rates taking a sudden downturn. That's when they panicked into action.

Loss of productivity and continuous hiring processes translate into substantial losses for organizations, most of which are not strong enough to survive the blow in addition to facing the external competition from other organizations in the industry. When the millennials join these organizations and do not find a favorable working environment their engagement levels are adversely affected and eventually they take the first opportunity to jump ship into organizations that are providing them with what they need. In short, you need to upgrade your talent management program to accommodate the things that motivate these millennials to give their best input to the organization.

Hence, it is an established fact that you need to redefine the parameters that define your human capital management. To make it more efficient and alluring for the millennials your talent management system needs a serious upgrade. Let's take a look at all what it should include. Remember, whatever we will be talking about here onwards is nothing new. You've read it all throughout the course of this book. This section is just like a refresher to jog your memory into recalling the important ingredients you need to cook a talent management program that will draw and retain the millennial talent to and in your organization.

A report titled *Millennial Careers: 2020 Vision* released by Manpower adequately sums up the things millennials look for when hunting for jobs. According to this report it is job security and money that tops the list for most; however, flexibility, holidays, and great people also form part of the priority list for these youngsters.

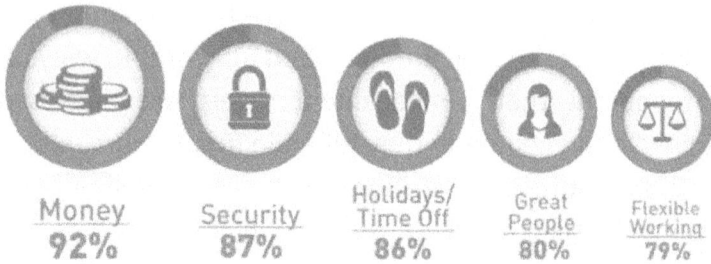

Money	Security	Holidays/ Time Off	Great People	Flexible Working
92%	87%	86%	80%	79%

TOP 5 PRIORITIES WHEN LOOKING FOR A JOB[31]

These priorities however, may vary from country to country, and within the United States they may differ from one state to another. The one thing that remains common is that these millennials 'need' the money to pay off their student loans that are weighing down on them

– they don't mind working for it, but they'll do so on their own terms.

Truth is that organizations need to come to terms with the fact that millennials are not looking for "jobs for life". They should be expected to change roles and even organizations throughout their careers as they quench their thirst of continuous learning and development. But there are millennials who remain loyal to their jobs and organizations – *what makes them stay?*

[31] Millennial Careers: 2020 Vision Report

The Deloitte Millennial Survey 2016[32] came up with a credible insight into this phenomenon. The image below shows the survey results as a relative measure of things that hold importance for millennials and eventually drive them to remain loyal to their organizations.

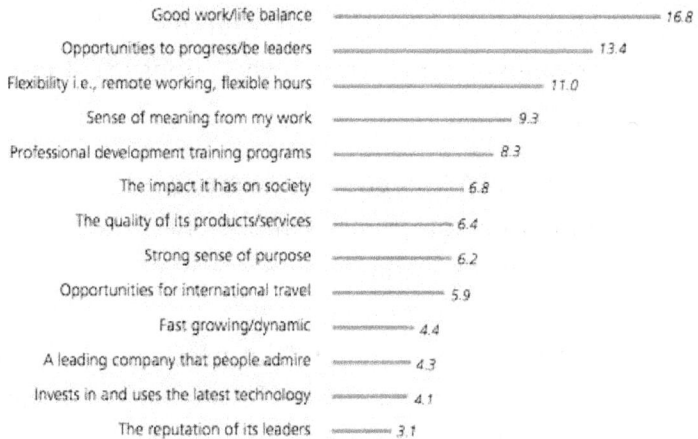

Good work/life balance —————————————————— 16.8
Opportunities to progress/be leaders ————————————— 13.4
Flexibility i.e., remote working, flexible hours ————————— 11.0
Sense of meaning from my work ———————— 9.3
Professional development training programs ————— 8.3
The impact it has on society ————— 6.8
The quality of its products/services ———— 6.4
Strong sense of purpose ———— 6.2
Opportunities for international travel ——— 5.9
Fast growing/dynamic —— 4.4
A leading company that people admire —— 4.3
Invests in and uses the latest technology — 4.1
The reputation of its leaders — 3.1

Q. For each of the following groups of four, please indicate what would be the strongest reason for choosing to work for an organization and what would be the weakest.

According to this survey, the strongest reason for millennials to remain in a company for longer durations is the good work/life balance, whereas the leaders' reputation came as the weakest factor. However, this survey did not include the monetary compensation and benefits as a potential factor – it was assumed to be a given factor.

[32] https://www2.deloitte.com/content/dam/Deloitte/global/Documents/About-Deloitte/gx-millenial-survey-2016-exec-summary.pdf

Considering these two surveys collectively, it is safe to assume that the millennials are looking for greater flexibility, they want holidays, and people that they can learn from. Something we have been pointing out since the beginning of this book. Handling millennials is not as difficult as organizations deem it to be. The only thing most challenging in our opinion is bringing about a permanent change in the way things are done within the organization.

As we wrap this book up, we believe we have provided you with a comprehensive insight into how millennials are inspiring a change in the way organizations manage the talent available to them. At this point, we feel it is necessary to emphasize the need for you to be smart enough and acknowledge the need of the hour. You need the millennials to work for you and continue to do so for longer than their usual stay in an organization. To make that happen you need to *"give some to gain some"*. Give the millennials what they want. Begin today. Even if it's gradual, it is important to set the process into motion. You'll eventually get where you want to be. Plus, once you get a hang of how to properly manage the skills inventory at your disposal, the journey will be one that is at a steady pace heading towards the destinations goals of the organization.

You've got everything you need in this book right here. These millennials, with their skills, knowledge, expertise, abilities, and innovative ideas can take your organization to greater height of success. You only have to provide them an environment that helps them flourish individually and professionally. Just set to work and make it happen!

ACKNOWLEDGEMENTS

This work would not have been possible without the support of a "village" as they say. I am grateful to all those whom I have had the pleasure to work with during this and other projects. Each and every member my close NFM family. Dr. Brooke Porter who has been very supportive and full of great ideas. I am especially indebted to Dr. Mary Goebel-Lundholm as my teacher and mentor, she has taught me more than I could ever give her credit for here. She has challenged me often times, stimulating my personal growth.

Nobody has been more important to me in the pursuit of this project than my friends my family.

ABOUT THE AUTHOR

Philipe Bruce holds professional degrees in Leadership, Organizational Management, Entrepreneurship and Economic Development and obtained further Certification in Organizational Development. He is very involved in the community around him and has served as a volunteer firefighter. The author later on founded P.O.D.S. Coaching, LLC and has mentored new entrepreneurs, intrapreneurs, and small businesses in Management, Professional and Organizational Development. He helped transform their business ideas into formal plans in addition to finding comprehensive solutions for regular organizational issues they face.

Philipe prides himself in being a forward thinker and has a go-getter approach at everything he undertakes. With great passion for human connections, Industrial Psychology, Personal and Organizational Development, he aims to learn and create a better understanding of the professional world and our place in it. This mission has cast him in many different roles: student, employee, entrepreneur, author, small business/organizational and personal development coaching across the globe.

Visit www.philipebruce.com for more on Philipe's work.

P.O.D.S.
Coaching, LLC

www.ingramcontent.com/pod-product-compliance
Lightning Source LLC
Chambersburg PA
CBHW060330200326
41519CB00011BA/1894